Fresh Courage
IN RETIREMENT
Finding purpose, essence and fulfillment

Explore the possibilities

Sharon Rolph, MA/ABS

IN RETIREMENT

Finding purpose, essence and fulfillment

Sharon Rolph, MA/ABS

Time is too slow for those who wait,
Too swift for those who fear,
Too long for those who grieve,
Too short for those who rejoice,
But for those who love,
time is Eternity.

- Henry van Dyke (1852-1933)

Fresh Courage
IN RETIREMENT

Finding purpose, essence and fulfillment

Published by EDK Books and
Distributed by EDK Distribution, LLC
edkbookdistribution.com
edkbooksanddistribution@gmail.com
(206) 227-8179

10 9 8 7 6 5 4 3 2

Printed in the United States of America

ISBN 978-1-7339618-9-9

Editor: Barbara Kindness

Cover Design & Layout: Julie K. Lee

TABLE OF CONTENTS

CHAPTERS

INTRODUCTION

12/10/20 After a big AHA!

I might be a little weird but I love to hear and read stories of people who've had a near-death experience. And, I marvel at the willingness of author and pastor Todd Burpo to listen and respect his young son Colton's experience in the *Heaven Is for Real* book and movie.

During the last three to four years, as I ponder the phrase in the Lord's Prayer "Thy will be done, on earth as it is in Heaven," I've actually started sensing that Heaven really *WANTS* to come to earth. So, I sometimes would imagine myself standing in Heaven, sensing all the beauty, fragrance, vibrancy, color, love and peace that people with Near-Death Experiences (NDE) talk about. Then, I wondered *HOW* would it change, impact or make life back here different. I'm now starting to understand how.

I had a huge AHA moment yesterday! Last week, I'd heard author Lewis Howes's interview with Rhonda Byrne, the author of *The Secret*, on his podcast. The show started out with her sound bite: "The more effortless you are, the greater you manifest everything that you ever dreamt of."

As I chewed on this, I really felt I am daily living an effortless life as I am growing my coaching business. Today, I operate from a sense of what my next step is, from a feeling deep inside. Like a still small voice—so I have to be intentional about listening—as opposed to being a goals-oriented person. I don't exactly know how to grow my business, but since I've come to respect the wisdom from inside, I trust the process of "knowing" when I need to know. And what I seem to need next shows up for me—within the hour, a day or two—like when I go to the second-hand store, or when someone gives me something at the right moment. I get a sense of being taken care of and synchronicity. How cool is that!!

So, the lightning bolt came when I realized my effortless vitality plan that I'd worked on all year during the pandemic of 2020 was to teach people how to discover, live and make new choices aligned with their DNA. That's living from their heart, where it flows effortlessly! Like the journey I've been on that feels like Heaven on earth. And another aha! happened earlier in the year that felt *so* good was understanding that I could actually be paid to live my life vision *and* recognize that the resulting feeling was to be in love with life! I *WANT* that for *YOU*, too.

I now stand on tippy toes for all my dreams to manifest. I have a confidence; it's just a matter of time. People need this. Just as important to me as my dream of being of service is my willingness to be the one to influence and speak out so you grow and realize your *own* dreams, your *own* Heaven on earth, as you create an ideal life, too. That's a huge shift from wanting *THINGS* (or money) to satisfy one's desires.

Why do I do what I do? I believe it can change the world! What's better than Heaven on earth? I'm a behavioral scientist and a retirement coach; a great, unique and perfect combination to deliver this message to you.

I believe there is a deep contentment, peace and satisfaction in knowing the reason you are here. Knowing you have a place to fit in. If you have focused commitment, a generous heart, and vibrant dreams you want to bring to life, I will guide and partner with you in uncovering your special DNA to understand and know fully your uniqueness so you thrive.

Does this sound good to you? Is this what you are looking for? I want to touch the desire you have to contribute and to matter. Like the feeling of petting your cat or dog and feeling connected, right? This is your most important day and place in life! I will help you find clarity so you have excitement and personal growth too.

Let's recover the excitement and curiosity of a three-year-old; feel the joy of exploring. Let's renew our appreciation for the mystery of life.

Ever watch in amazement at someone whose job fits them like a glove? Maybe it's been a waiter/waitress in your favorite restaurant. Maybe it's your favorite singer or actor. Maybe it's the daycare worker or teacher? Self-discovery is amazing. *THIS* can be you.

On the following pages, along with what I am learning on my journey are the thoughts, determinations, and discoveries shared by many accomplished people in our contemporary world. At the end of the book,

I have offered a segment inviting you to GO DEEPER in each chapter with additional valuable resources for you to explore on your own. My podcasts with contributors are listed so you can go into more depth on a particular topic.

Let's get started.

PREFACE

Be Fulfilled

You might wonder why I chose these chapter titles. I had a couple of people recommend author Donald Miller to me as being a model to study. I was quite impressed with his book *Scary Close*. How real, vulnerable and engaging he was, as the book is about being single and terrible at relationships! Then, I read his *Building a StoryBrand: Clarify Your Message So Customers Will Listen*. His style is clear and simple.

Miller says what people want pretty much falls into seven categories. Among them are to be safe, healthy, happy and strong, etc. I connect these same desires to living a better life in retirement—actually, to any season of life! So my chapter titles examine these same topics.

Also, I probably need to explain something else up front: I do not live my life based on fear. Period.

Here's my story.

When I moved across country from Washington State to Tampa, Florida, for a job transfer, my friends had told me to allow three to six months to find a new community and friends. I felt I was chugging along pretty well about month four. Then I lost it! Started doubting the process and dancing with homesickness.

Before moving, I'd felt a strong sense that this was the 'right' move for me and that God was teaching me a new thing about love; sensing a feeling of being a newborn baby being rocked in His arms, like starting over!

So, if this *was* my right path, going home after four months wasn't right! I was going to need some help. And, looking up Scriptures on fear and courage proved interesting. I found three references in a short amount of space in Joshua: 1:6—be strong and of a good courage; 1:7—Only be thou strong and very courageous; 1:9 and 1:18—be strong and very courageous.

I remember stomping my foot and talking to myself about being strong and brave, of good courage, very courageous, bold and strong. Lots of days. Lots of times. Need I say again that I *REFUSE* to live my life based on *FEAR?* It solidified my resolve to give no place in my mind and heart to "what if's" or worry or anxiety or drama!

I am very saddened with all the fear in the TV media: the news, the ads, the shows, the commentators! It's possible to buy insurance for all sorts of things (to protect your fears, your pets, etc.). I noticed when the pharmaceuticals ads started saying, "*when* you see your doctor," "*when* you have a UTI," or "*when* you get the flu…." What happened to *IF, not when*?!! Brainwashing??

Another thing: My favorite verse is Ephesians. 3:20 (NIV): Now to Him who is able to do immeasurably more than all we ask or imagine, according to His power that is at work within us.

Years ago, in doing a word study on biblical terms for power, I found two versions of power in this one verse. *Dynamis* power (like dynamite) means miraculous power, mighty or Holy Spirit. And, *energeo,* meaning energy, active, be at work, operative, powerful, effective.

Also, in Ephesians. 1:19 and 3:7, this says to me that we can co-create with God: my energy *and* His miracle power. The ideal. The DNA He created in me and the work of my hands being a dynamite combination to do *explosively* good stuff.

Your work + your DNA coming together for jobs that fit you like a glove & are fulfilling! That's the kind of work I do!

FRESH COURAGE

FRESH COURAGE:

You're the boss now

CHAPTER ONE

Conserve Resources

It's a NEW DAY. You are retired or are anticipating to be, soon. It's a 'Get Out of Jail' free day! The endless pajama days. Oh, the FREEDOM! And, my, oh my, lots of SLEEP!

It's the day you become the boss of you! The day you call your own shots. You decide *when* to get up. *Why* you get up. And how *to* start the day. What makes your time important today? How will you bring the best of who you are to this moment? It's your time to shine! What will bring you satisfaction?

To be honest, the stress of life has aged you. The responsibilities aged you. Worry aged you. Your commute stole your calm and sleep from you. Ah, now for the freedom to sleep all you want! This is good and could last for two or three months. Then what?

When your job is gone, what hobbies and pastimes have you had that you can now give more time to? What volunteering have you wished you had time for? Which friends do you want to spend more time with? Do you have books waiting to be read? Or songs you want to write or sing or play?

So you don't get lost, I want to walk alongside you in these next few chapters as you recall the passions, dreams and wishes you've had over the years. You are one-of-a-kind. Your desires mean something. They're in your heart. They matter. Turn up the burner on the things that once mattered to you and then got buried over the years by responsibilities. They may have changed. Be curious again. Love what's in your heart.

You see, life marches on and becomes monotonous sometimes. Since 18.9 percent of us Boomers don't have any children and grandkids, that part of retirement, where lots of people are pulling on us for our time, attention and favors, is mostly missing for us. The threat of becoming isolated and depressed is quite real. In fact, folks in my local senior center told me they are combatting isolation, depression and declining health. This won't be your case, 'cause I will help you make better, healthier, more vibrant choices.

Fresh Courage is what we have when we've taken a new view of life after a vacation or a wonderful trip or been with a dear friend. It comes with that contented, settled, clear-headed feeling. Our spirit wakes up in pleasure. We are able to make better decisions and call the shots that make us happy. Pay attention and honor what your heart desires. You may not realize *why* you desire what you do, but give it attention. Its message will come to you.

Being happy, loving life and finding joy, in my opinion, is nearly "Heaven on earth." Using your natural talent, gifts and strengths are also often keys to your joy. You are enough. You are valued!

I love inspiring and encouraging people. I also lose track of time when I sew. Over the years, I've collected words of wisdom. So, when I started quilting, I realized I also loved working with color. At one of my temporary jobs in Texas at a JOANN Fabrics store, we were taught to ask people what project they were working on. Even now, as a customer, I still like asking people what they are working on. That's when a postal letter carrier told me she made fabric postcards for various holidays for friends. That particular day was Halloween. A couple of weeks later, I realized how my words of wisdom, love of color and sewing could all come together to inspire others with postcard-size fabric art.

I really want you to be on a quest to *realize* what makes you happy. The first coaching book I read from our recommended reading list was *The JOY Diet* by Martha Beck. It made such an impact on me. In fact, I'll go so far as to say it could transform you, too.

I was profoundly moved by the first chapter as it got me in touch with the wisdom I have inside. I take seriously the need to take care of myself first, before my clients. There are so many fun and delightful ways to feed the spirit and soul. What I learned is how serious a business it is to treat myself well every day and to honestly desire what I want.

One of the things deep in my heart is to be fully using all the gifts I've been given. I feel very responsible to use them for the purpose for which they were meant. You see, I don't want to stand before God and have to admit that I buried *any* of them! I don't want that for you, either.

Would you be willing to be curious about what your talents are and how they could be used to serve others? (We change, when our brain lights up!) When I realized that I could get paid to use my talents while living my joy in service to others, it seemed like Heaven on earth. Wow! Really? How IDEAL!

So, wouldn't you rather decide to live from your heart, use your talent, and serve others, since you're the boss now and it's your time to shine? We've got untold years and decades yet to live. I wonder if it's possible to find fulfillment and meaning along the way that make our heart sing? Time flies when we are having fun.

Time is marching on. Use it wisely. Refuse to become bored, confused or aimless. I'm here so you *don't* spend two to five years to get focused or to find your new center. I've collected lots of possible resources for you to explore. Perhaps listening to some of the fifty-plus podcasts I made while you drive or walk will inspire possibilities, too. (One of my favorites is with Joyce Major, author of *Smiling at the World,* which I'll tell you more about later.) The Internet puts a world of information at our fingertips. Explore.

This past year or two I've worked on loving and honoring myself more. As a single, never-married woman longing to be cherished and waiting, and waiting, this was BIG. It's made such a difference! When I started reminding myself, "I'm doing the best I can," it shut up the critical or judging voice in my head! Whew! Stop judging or comparing yourself so much! You could do this too, couldn't you?

Self-care is often a low priority, but it certainly matters. Just buying a rose or small bouquet helps me be more in love with life. I'm getting better at decluttering and am surprised at the impact it has on my sense of me, too. It's another method of self-love.

In *Love Money, Money Loves You*, British author/teacher Sarah McCrum says to love everything. So, one morning, I was putting on my slippers and the thought, Do I love my slippers? popped up. *Sorta.* I turned to my closet and again a new thought, *Do I love my clothes? Yeah.* Then, a real kicker came to mind, *Do I love my body? Not really.* It's another version of loving myself, loving life, on a deeper level. It seemed to change me, ever so slightly.

Why talk about this? Well, it's all part of becoming a better version of ourselves in this new stage of life.

When you prepared for retirement, most of the focus and planning were centered on your finances—your money. As a behavioral scientist, I'm focusing on all the *other* factors of this transition: social, mental, emotional and spiritual changes that may not have come up in any conversations as yet. I once saw a facilitator ask her workshop attendees, "What do you get from your job, besides a paycheck?" Their list of thirty to forty things is an example of the 'rest of the story.'

Then, as we switch from saving to spending those savings, everything becomes real, and the focus becomes conserving resources. The reality of, "Did I save enough?" or doubting if you have what it takes, or even faking "good enough," begins to roam through your mind. Perhaps as an elder, you feel it's time to be taken care of? Don't hold your breath here, right?

I'm right there with you. I don't live my life based on fear so worry and anxiety rarely come to mind. But I'm right there with you making the shoes last a while longer, turning the thermostat a little lower, and stretching the grocery budget—these become the new normal. But, again, it isn't based on fear. Stretching resources kinda becomes a game, instead.

I attended my first year of college on a Work-Study program. College and employment happened together, usually with night and weekend classes all the way through getting my master's degree. Years later, I took a leap of faith to leave a secure job that resulted in a series of jobs where I started at the bottom-of-the-ladder. Another time, in between jobs, I lived totally off my credit cards! So, "stretching resources" and I know each other well.

But there is another way! Your job or career probably didn't engage all of your talents: also known as under-employment. Now that you are your own boss, there's nobody stopping you. Let's get serious about taking an inventory of all your resources that may have been hidden or underutilized.

Would you allow me to inspire you and start a few *I wonder if it's possible…?* thoughts to awaken in you? Please? Was there ever a time you had a dream or two? Perhaps a quiet little idea or thought happened while on vacation. While you were breathing deeply and gazing at the stars, the beach or a fireplace; when there was a sense of contentedness about you.

Could be, your creative side is waiting for you to act on the ideas that have already popped up. Once we turn a deaf ear, the messages/ideas stop!! Turn your heart muscle on again; promise you won't ignore it this time. Listen intently for the possibilities. Get curious. Get grateful. Listen to your heart.

Whenever I got an idea as a teenager that seemed too much, it would scare me. "I couldn't do *THAT*" would be my response. Since I lived on a farm, I imagined it would be like stepping off the back of a flatbed truck. I could really get *hurt*!

Then a curious thing happened. A couple of weeks later, the idea would come back and it still seemed scary, but this time my response was, "I could still twist my ankle even going down an eighteen-inch step!"

But by the time the idea came up a third time, I was finally willing to embrace the risk. Does this sound anything like you? Now, I realize, I was responding to God speaking to my spirit and awakening me to "what's possible."

My personal retirement plan was to work until I turned seventy. However, eighteen months prior, a reorganization created a pivot point in my life, so I opted to pursue a career growth opportunity into a coaching program. As it turned out, in mid-April, I started coaching school and the next week I said goodbye to my previous job, ending a long-standing career. The next three months were filled with paperwork: insurance, Social Security and Medicare options. Once that settled down, I started wondering how I would know if I was being productive or if I was just wasting time? Being efficient and effective had always been important to me.

After a few days, I recalled a tool we created in the first coaching class—my Essence statement. It was powerful, deeply embracing and acknowledging who I am on the inside—like my inner voice; my true self. By this time, I'd created a colorful fabric wall hanging of my Essence statement. So I began to read it two or three times a day to help me answer the question: "How am I going to be productive" today? Here it is: I am a precious jewel of wisdom. I am a colorful collaborator, learner and motivator. I am tranquil, authentic and a pure inspirer. I light fire!

Gradually, I realized it helped to center me. Whenever I lived from my Essence, I'd know each day would be good, right and "productive." It was like putting on a new jacket, owning this new me; this new awareness, new life, and being true to my best. Good.

About six to eight months into the coursework, I returned from a lunch break and said to no one in particular, "It's not okay to be invisible" as I stomped my foot and slapped a table. WOW! Where did that come from? I surprised myself! Now, years later, I recognize it as the beginning of my caterpillar to butterfly transformation process.

As an introvert and middle child of five, being invisible came naturally. I didn't want to rock the boat and get in trouble growing up, so I got good grades and was always obedient. So not being seen was sort of a good thing. Besides, my sister got the kind of attention that repulsed me. So, life was OK. Then buckling down to college, work, apartments, cars, furniture, bills etc. in the rhythm of being responsible for my shelter, education and travel, my only self-expression had come from sewing and baking.

Expecting growth at work initially came passively, believing my boss would advance me "in time." In time, I sought out opportunity to grow through ToastMasters training and Dale Carnegie courses to prepare myself for more.

The steps to be seen were gentle, slow, careful. Yet I did take some risky choices and express my individuality thanks to my sense of adventure.

One of my favorite extracurricular ventures has been singing, so I went to the national quartet convention in Nashville (yes, Elvis was in the house), and to Australia as a member of a church choir tour. But at work, as an introvert, being steady, reliable and responsible in a logical, professional way was accepted, expected and normal progress.

The one big risk at work to be seen came when I had a boss who encouraged me to try any new idea I came up with. He created a safe space for me. The day I showed him my fabric art blocks was a daring and vulnerable moment. I was nervous and scared! And shocked, when he didn't shoot it down, but left the door open to see where I'd go with it.

When an opportunity to participate in an employee involvement event on the production floor came, I created a series of art blocks with one-liners based on trust in teams and turned them into display posters! I stuck my neck out and lived to tell about it. Whew!

Another risk was giving a ten-minute speech before managers of employee-involvement teams, daring to speak the truth and challenge them on the future of our empowerment program.

So, after stomping my foot in the classroom, there wasn't any big behavior change on my part until a year later. I'd decided to give myself a 70th birthday party and my theme was Becoming Visible—my coming out party! Complete with a speech.

But the one photo that most expresses 'becoming visible' to me was taken later at a Christmas party. I'd started a Meetup group six months before and about twenty-five people came to our first party. When they raised their glasses and made a toast to *ME*, I was deeply touched! You see, *I* was the reason they'd met each other and they were expressing their gratitude! I still cherish that moment!

My message here is that it takes courage, vulnerability and heart to let others see our unique gifts, contributions, our dreams and passions. When we no longer have a title, a business card, a job or career, yet we have an affluence of time, we get the opportunity and have freedom to live from our hearts; to express what's in our hearts and contribute from our passion and love of life. What could be more satisfying and rewarding than that?

Allow me to introduce you to my second-ever podcast guest, award-winning author and champion volunteer Joyce Major, whom I met through someone in the Meetup group!

In her words, "Jumping out of my life, my shoes, my houseboat, and my career, I decided to celebrate my life with the gift of freedom for a full year and perhaps, just maybe, do a bit of good along the way."

Joyce claims she's a slow adjuster, not a great tourist. She wanted to have time to actually unpack her suitcase, know where she was, and get a chance to know people. And she wanted to volunteer. Not having traveled much, every single country was an option, so the hard part was narrowing down the choices! She wanted to visit each continent and country for at least a month, visit someplace that would challenge her, that had something to do with wildlife, and where room and board and transportation would cost less than $25,000 for the full year. (Room and board for short-term volunteer trips go everywhere from free to a couple thousand dollars per volunteer, since the wildlife projects are trying to keep their projects alive.)

I asked Jane, "Did you always feel safe?"

Now, Joyce was fifty-seven at the time, and anytime she told someone she was volunteering, people were always gracious; however, on her journey, she watched other women in each different culture to see how they walked, their eye contact with strangers, their hand motions, and she learned to mimic them. Since many of the other volunteers were right out of college, she was often known as Mama, and even often made chocolate chip cookies for them!

Here are a couple of my favorite stories she tells.

"I was teaching English in China at a high school, and you have to picture seventy kids in the classroom back then. They're all perfectly polite. They're just lovely. And I'm trying to get them to speak out loud, which was very challenging. I had no books. It was all oral. I started writing songs up on the board. The songs that had the best words were Beatles songs from my generation. I wrote the words to my favorite song, 'Imagine,' and went through the verses. First, I said it, and then they said it, and then I said it again. I told them that this was one of my favorite songs. And then the kids, who typically didn't raise their hand, asked me to do something. They asked me to sing it!

"It was a shock. Oh dear. Okay. Okay. Okay. I don't sing, but I love that song. And they wanted to hear my favorite song. (I usually do people a really big favor and don't sing out loud in a crowd!) Because they asked, it's like, okay, let's hit it. Bravely, I sang it, though it was hard not to tear up because they were all looking at me and I'm singing about peace, singing about the world that I love. And I got through it all glassy-eyed and probably ready to tear up. And then I said, 'How about you?'

'Is there somebody that would want to sing?'

"There's a shyness in those classrooms. Nobody wants to stand out. Pure silence. I couldn't get anybody to raise their hand, but all the kids looked at this one boy who was sitting toward the back of the room. He nodded. He was, like, okay, I will sing it. And all he had heard was my weak rendition. I had given him enough of the tune that he carried it, and his English was good enough that he could say all the words.

"He stood up and he sang the most beautiful version of 'Imagine' I've ever heard. His voice was heavenly. It absolutely brought me to bursting with joy. I was, like, okay, now I'm in full-on tears. I couldn't hold them back. That moment was absolutely one of my all-time favorite experiences. It was beautiful. It was wonderful."

I love when magic moments like that happen. You too might find something amazing happen in a new situation, just by singing a song because it is heartfelt.

Joyce continued: "I think that's the thing with volunteering. Unexpected things happen. I didn't know. I hadn't any idea what volunteering at each one of these projects would be like, but unexpected things kept happening, and those opened me up and I got to see myself in a different way. I got to experience something that was, like, *Oh, look at Joyce, you sang*! And this boy sang who was not going to sing before this. He wasn't going to stand up and be a solo artist. He had a beautiful voice.

"Another experience happened when I volunteered with the baboons. My joke was that teaching middle school prepared me. When I looked at volunteering with baboons, I was, like, I can do that! There's a big problem in South Africa.

"Baboons—they are, well, they're smart. They'd rather go into your house and get fast food from your cupboards than forage in the bush. And they'll invade. If you leave a window open, they all go inside. The whole troop! They'll go through your cupboards. They'll go through your fridge, eat what they want, and then they leave a mess behind. Of course, that behavior creates a lot of animosity with people, who would rather get rid of the baboons. My job was to keep the baboons in the woods. Every day I'd sit out in the field with two South African guys, and we would try to keep the baboons where they were supposed to be.

"The most interesting thing about that project was sitting with two black guys from South Africa talking to them about what it was like with apartheid and how things are different now. Meanwhile, the woman who had started this project came by and said, 'I'm going to go check on the baboons. Do you want to come with?' And I'm like, 'Yeah, I want to come with. Sure.' *I'll be Jane Goodall!* She said, 'Okay, well just follow me, do what I do.' And I'm thinking, *okay, I will follow you.*

"So, we're tiptoeing through the woods. I'm following her exactly. I don't want to upset anybody because George was the dominant male, and he was up in a tree and he's big. We came to this little hill and we sat down to watch the young baboons that were playing in the river down below. The other bigger baboons surrounded us. These are *wild baboons*. And I was telling myself, *okay, I'm fine. She's here. I'm fine.*

"Then suddenly one baboon decided he liked me, I guess. He approached me from behind and started grooming my hair and I'm confused. *Okay, what do I, what do I do now?*

"And the lady said, 'Well, let me know if it hurts.' And I'm picturing that he's going to take a big chunk of my hair and yank it out. And then I'm going to have to figure out how long it's going to take for that patch of missing hair to grow back.

"But that's not what happened. He groomed me with his ten little fingers, so nicely, gently, and apparently, did not find any bugs, which was also good. He groomed my head like I was a baboon. That experience was totally unexpected. I was floored. Okay, this is amazing, you know, a wild baboon is grooming my hair. So, things unexpected, totally unexpected happened throughout my year."

I asked Joyce why that experience was so significant for her. Was it because wild animals tend to be fierce, but this one was kind of loving?

"Yeah, he was. He was loving and had absolutely nothing on his agenda, but oh, I'm going to take care of you, you need your hair done. Then he gave me a little hug. I will always remember his sweet little fingers wrapped around my arm.

"I think another part of all the wildlife sanctuaries is that the animals were so loved, well-taken-care-of, and the people who started these projects to help them were so passionate. You know, it was so wonderful, so inspiring to be around passionate people who were all charged up with what they wanted to create and to make change in the world. And it was contagious. Oh, this way of life was a beautiful, fresh look at the world. And I saw how the world could be if I lived with that kind of passion.

"Volunteering was a refresher. It was like if you went to a beauty store and they gave you a facial—the best facial ever— and you felt like you had a whole new skin.

"It was like, look, oh my gosh, I have a whole new heart. I felt so much love from so many different places."

It was clear that Joyce's personal reward for being courageous was that her heart was expanded as she learned lasting lessons from these animals. What else?

"I think I got a better sense of who I am, which is interesting that at age fifty-seven, I still didn't know. But I saw myself in all these different environments and saw how I was accepted. I really loved learning that being someplace where I didn't know how to do things was good for me. I didn't know how to feed monkeys or make their food for them. And I didn't know how to teach Chinese kids English. And when I was a reporter in Ireland, for certain I didn't know how to write a story. My personal rewards were vast.

"I came back refreshed. It's like I had gotten this whole beautiful feeling of what the world is like, and I was so proud of myself for actually being brave enough to travel the world for a year. Now if I can only get everybody out and doing something they don't know how to do.

"I was doing all these new things and I was totally uncomfortable, but people were kind to me. All the people at these volunteer projects were gentle. The kindness that they gave me was good for me.

"My intuition told me that my growth needed to come from being out in the world. I needed to see different cultures. I needed to see what was important in different cultures; how they responded to each other; how they loved each other.

"That's what I needed. My little soul was saying, *Go Do* that choice. I think that's the thing. Whatever melody people hear from their souls, we need to listen. And know what the melody is. Then I think we get our soul happy, and we can feel good. We need to question. Wow. How would it work for me? Relate to your being a learner and paying attention to how the other cultures affect who you are. Even the animals. What can I learn from an animal?

"I feel a part of the world now. Going to Third World countries, I saw the joy that people create by living in the day. I will never forget the smiles in South Africa and how they were present with me. I mean, I could just talk to them and we looked at each other and the same thing actually happened in a lot of places where we were just in the day. And it made me think that when I'm back here, I'm not always in the day. Maybe I was thinking about what was going to come next, or maybe I'm thinking about what just happened, but how often am I really looking at somebody and saying, *I'm with you, right here.*

"And the trip had a profound effect on my spending. Having more, getting more, spending more, earning more all became less important. Life became about finding passion, in helping others, and figuring out how to be in the moment more often."

Joyce Major's children's book, *The Orangutan Rescue Gang* is a perfect adventure book for 5th graders. (For your volunteering trip-planning process, try these websites: HELPX.net www.VFP.org www.wwoof.net)

After hearing Joyce's story, could it be possible you are ready now? Think of all those amazing resources at your fingertips now. Perhaps the limitations from the past aren't in the picture now, anyway. I wonder if it's possible to turn your focus on engaging your latent resources. To become fully seen?

Maybe being a volunteer is not calling you at the moment—at least not on a global scale. There are plenty of opportunities right at your doorstep seeking your help and a good start.

ACTIONS TO TAKE

- Prime the pump with a list of things that give you pleasure and joy. Start as young as you can remember. (I was surprised one day after coming back from being away over a weekend that when I went to water my geraniums and petunias, I became aware that growing them gave me joy!)

- Make another list of things you are grateful for.

- Recall over your life people you've admired. Make a list of six to eight people, alive or who have passed on. What is/was it about them you admired?

- Imagine you are unleashing not only your heart but also your joy!! Entertaining the possibilities and being curious adds a new component to your days. What could be possible?

HIGH5 TEST – It's https://high5test.com/ – applying positive psychology strengths and discovering what you are naturally good at.

Could it be that ignoring your heart is also ignoring your source of joy and creativity? Let's trade your caution for curiosity. I sometimes wonder if depression is our spirit being disappointed in our holding ourselves back.

- Perhaps take a risk. Listen to your heart.

What matters with spending money now is being careful, but not worried; being honest but not tight. Accept help or find other ways to give birthday gifts. Don't invite ANY negative "what-if" games to trouble you. Besides, worry just wastes brain power and heartbeats. One of my favorite lines is, "Worry is a misuse of imagination"—Dan Zadra.

The unknowns are the things that most often challenge our resources now. What happens if we didn't save enough? What if I fall? What if I can't be there for my granddaughter's wedding, or I need to take a trip? I wonder if more gifts could be made or written, instead of bought. Maybe I can alternate years for taking trips or seeing the kids.

CHAPTER TWO

Conserving Time

I've long held a distaste for commercials and advertising. To me, it borders on brainwashing. Yes, we might need new information but the repetition and "in your face" distraction is mostly offensive to me. (You know, I heard you the *first* time!)

Or, it's a temptation that I'm already trying hard to ignore. And using loud, fast-talking people assures me it's *your* priority, not mine. In fact, in 2020, I found even the news could feel jarring and unwelcome. Besides the isolation, home alone, and canceled plans, life was frustrating more than ever.

Now as I am focused on writing, the distractions and Black Friday ads are everywhere, making it very tough to focus.

Conserving your time and attention from wasted distractions to focus on what's important is what really matters. Focus is healthy. What's the point to conserve time, when we live with time affluence? First, and a major point, is to combat boredom, depression, or feeling lost. Is sending emails to your grandson(s) what matters? Daily, weekly or monthly? Is learning your new instrument or language what matters? You decide. Is contributing to your community (being seen and visibly present, even virtually) what matters?

To me, it's healthier to trust and believe that my resources of time and money will work out fine. Sure, it's trusting the process without fear. I've been reminding myself often that when angels appear in the Bible, their first words are usually 'Fear Not'! Or messages from people who have died sent back messages of "don't worry, I'm fine!"

Be generous with the time you spend with others. Don't hide or disappear. Sharing your garden, your viewpoint, your flowers, your stories or feelings and wisdom usually is a delight, actually for both of you.

I've been blessed with looking a lot younger than people expect. So maybe I'm not affected as much as others who feel age discrimination. Or, because I don't expect it, I don't experience it? Boomers have been impacting the world and breaking the mold as we age. But retirement is ripe for a massive culture change. Where's the Opportunity/Needs Repository database for us to find what the community would like help with, *anyway*?

In *What Retirees Want,* by Dr. Ken Dychtwald, the author lists many opportunities for employers to improve their policies on aging to take *advantage* of our wisdom, experiences, and talent supply.

On the other hand, Dr. Ken says there's collectively 195 billion hours of leisure time a year for those 65+. This equates to 3.9 trillion hours over the next twenty years. (WOW!)

Boomers are now time affluent for the first time in their adult life. Time that's looking for fun, stimulating, nourishing, purposeful, even transformative, things to do. Dr. Ken's research team was fascinated that Americans see retirement as "a whole new chapter in life"—a starting point.

The word 'consequential' is defined as following a result or effect, or the nature of a secondary result. So, when my mother told me helping others made them feel good, what was convincing was when she said I'd feel good *too*: consequential happiness.

Other consequences: We plant a garden for the by-product of having fresh salads on our dinner table, right? We study for our classes *so that* we pass the tests, learn and get good grades.

What could *you* do in the pursuit of happiness? Share your garden produce with neighbors? Let's become intentional about what we are doing, and could do, to be pursuing happiness on a daily basis, and not let it be mindlessly forgotten.

I intend to live my life dream *so that* I'm in love with Life. What is that for me? My happiness comes from the joy of unleashing the dreams of others all over the world.

Could you begin to see a positive *consequential happiness* in being a listener to your weird neighborhood kids or a senior living alone? Perhaps a consequential happiness could come from leaving a legacy. Maybe a legacy of happiness, even. How about it?

The American Association of Retired Persons (AARP) and senior centers are certainly helping to provide choices but there's room for so much more. Opportunities to solve significant problems and improve our neighborhoods. Develop activities for those who most need a break or change of scene—like widows and caregivers.

The Peace Corps created a whole new Boomer opportunity; now, I think it's time to reenlist. I want to see billboards asking Boomers 'what are you doing to advance your favorite charity: time, talent, passion, or finances?' By the same token, what are foundations doing to actively engage these billions of hours of leisure time. BOY! There's a marketing opportunity waiting to be solved!

I wonder if it's possible that you and I can help change this? If we can see the need, we can become curious enough to collaborate. I believe it's possible. In fact, I think it's magical and may create new knowledge, too.

Look, I don't want you wasting months and years feeling aimless and bored until you find your new focus. Let's not watch time slipping away and making room for despair and distractions. I believe we each have a golden nugget inside of us that the world is waiting for. However, confusion can kick in and we sometimes forget who we are without a job to go to, or a task to do and teammates and colleagues to partner with. This is when you need to remember who you are; the expert whatever, the college graduate, the bean counter extraordinaire. You are still that first chair trombone player from high school days who could wow the crowds again, maybe this time at the senior center or in an assisted living lobby. With my process and encouragement, you'll find your place to fit in, to matter and to make a difference; to focus early on in your new season. Socially giving and contributing keeps us alive mentally and spiritually.

It's true, older people may not be as esteemed as we'd like to be, or visible, or heard, but that doesn't give us license to be silent or not try or care. Putting in your two cents may be the wisdom someone needs to hear and help turn the tide in favor of the Good. Honor your wisdom first, so others can also.

Now, transitions can be confusing. That is normal. And focus could be tough at times. Help yourself. Remember birthdays and anniversaries by using a calendar to schedule them. They are important. Calendars help with focus, too. Put important events or seasonal chores on a calendar. Annual exams for eyes, ears and hearing.

It helps to think of the value of time by using Stephen Covey's Time Management Matrix. Is this task necessary, like chores? Is it a distraction, like emails and Facebook? Is it a waste, like TV and gaming and gossip? What's weird is that being productive is important, but *not* urgent, like learning, planning and preparing. So, the value of time could be measured by the importance of making a difference or leaving a legacy or preventing someone from failing in their studies! What an achievement and satisfaction that would bring!

Another podcast guest of mine was John Barnett, executive director of the US Educational Commission in Japan, exchanging scholars under the Fulbright programs, and past president for AARP for Washington State. His motto is "Live long, die short," motivated by a Stanford doctor's lecture. He posed a question for my audience: If you have volunteered with the same organization for several years, what makes you continue to volunteer there?

John shared his nine "Suggestions for Successful Volunteering".

He began by sharing: "At age sixty, I had a diagnosis of cancer and I was kind of motivated to work with people who have problems or health problems. I took the Stephen Ministries course, and was a lay chaplain in an inpatient hospice center for ten years as a volunteer every Monday. They had fifteen beds and I would make the rounds talking and listening to people. But this is pretty heavy work. So, to lighten up, I decided to become an Arboretum volunteer. Seattle has a very big Arboretum and Botanical Garden as well."

"The University of Washington's Forestry Department gave training every Saturday for four months—three hours every Saturday—on woody plants and flowers, about which I previously knew nothing. It was fun to take those courses. I met a lot of nice people, led children and adults as I told them about all of our wonderful plants in the Northwest. It was socialization for me and it was less of a load."

Tip #1: *Just start somewhere or try something.*

There are so many opportunities in America for volunteering. It's been said many times that America couldn't accomplish all the good that we are accomplishing without a lot of volunteers and AARP, which I love. Find something that you really enjoy. Where do you think you might want to volunteer—helping people with animals, walking their dog for them, or working in a kennel, or maybe you want to do like I did. I started by visiting people in a nursing home.

I found when I was volunteering—especially for people who had problems and this could be that they are now living in a nursing home or they just had a loved one pass away—it made them happier when I would listen to them and try to help them in some way. And it made *me* happy because I was seeing that I was apparently doing some good. I thought my purpose, at that time, was and still is, to some extent, to help people who are needy. It's very satisfying.

Tip #2: *Listen and learn.*

So, since I was diagnosed with cancer twenty-eight years ago, in order to stay well, I get up about four-thirty every morning, go to the health club, shower and have breakfast at home with my wife so that I stay active and engaged. I volunteer for four organizations and have a fulfilling life. A cancer support group got me interested in end-of-life issues, where I developed a specialty, in a sense, at the hospice center. I didn't have to say a lot. If you ask people what did you do in life or something like that, they're very anxious to tell you. Or, what made them happy about their kids and that sort of thing. So, it was really a good ear that was needed sometimes.

Tip #3: *Spread yourself around doing a variety of things.*

I also am a Japanese garden guide at the Arboretum, which is fun too because I speak Japanese and it was a kind of a natural thing for me. If you are going to stay with it, any organization will want you to have fun. A good volunteer organization will train you. Another advantage is that volunteering can turn into becoming a job.

Tip #4: *Be open to learning even more.*

I saw an opportunity to be a long-term care ombudsman. There are several kinds of ombudsman, but the kind I volunteered with—for which I took thirty-two hours of training that they provided at no cost to me— was to go into nursing homes, assisted living, and adult family homes to see if the residents' needs were being met. A lot of times I've found that they weren't being met. After a while, I became good enough that I was asked to go to the state capital in Olympia occasionally to meet with the Department of Social and Health Services to give advice on how to work successfully or volunteer successfully in these licensed facilities: namely nursing homes, assisted living communities, and adult family homes.

What I'm saying is that one of my big desires is lifelong learning and the volunteer organizations are great learning opportunities.

Tip #5: *Consider the social aspects.*

I think volunteers are generally pretty nice people and a lot of them have had quite a successful work life before they retired and became volunteers. We exchange information. One guy I met has bicycled in about thirty countries around the world, including Nepal and Switzerland. Another guy was in the Navy when they tested one of the atom bombs. He didn't get radioactive, I guess, because he's ninety-two now so he's survived quite well.

I was paired up with a doctor that I had had for fifteen years who had become an AARP volunteer. We got to talking on a new kind of basis when we worked together and shared our backgrounds. He didn't know much about me except from a medical point of view. Unless you shared some common activities, you now learn things you never knew. When you learn at these serendipitous moments, it's like the icing on the cake, making the experience all the richer and rewarding. And it's all a surprise 'cause that's part of the reward of socializing and working with other people.

Tip #6: *You'll live longer as volunteering improves your health.*

It's been proven that volunteering has positive effects on social and psychological factors, your personal sense of purpose and accomplishment. Plus, it enhances your social network, which can help to prevent stress and reduce disease. We know that by volunteering, you can lower your blood pressure. (The State with the greatest number of volunteers, proportionately, is Utah, and they're pretty healthy people.) The area with the fewest volunteers is the Southeastern United States. They also have the poorest health. And, volunteering gets me out and forces me to be physically active.

Tip #7: *Take a risk.*

Columnist David Brooks said that average people feel alienated from government. I had never talked to an elected official until I was seventy. I didn't go to Olympia to the State Capitol to do anything. By taking the risk of talking to my Senator, though I didn't feel comfortable, I realized I was doing something good for the adult population in Washington State. And I found out that it was okay. It led me to make other political contacts. Now I go to Olympia at least once or twice every legislative session and talk to my elected officials about what is needed, particularly for older adults and in our State.

There are other ways that you can kind of stick your neck out. I found out it wasn't as uncomfortable as I thought it would be, as a lay chaplain. In fact, I looked forward to my weekly visits to hospice. So, take a risk and see if you can grow from it. See if you can learn from it. If it's not your game, then try something else. What goes along with that is to get out of your own comfort zone and continue to grow in a way you might not have even planned on.

I say it takes a lot of courage to transition into retirement. Doing something new and continuing to learn, you're in charge of that. Look in the mirror. That's who's responsible for that.

Tip #8: *Anything is possible when you help others.*

AARP is leading in cybercrime- and fraud prevention. The organization helps people be better drivers and get insurance discounts. Then there's AARP tax aid. These are volunteers who are trained to do simple tax returns for people for free; particularly for a lot of immigrants who don't speak English very well. They look very happy because it was done and they didn't have to pay for it. We also have information on affordable housing, public transportation, employment. I'm teaching people how to do advanced directives.

If you go to the website, https://createthegood.aarp.org/ or https://www.aarp.org/volunteer/, you will have an opportunity to see what's available in your neighborhood and how far you're willing to travel.

Tip #9: *You get a chance to improve the quality of life of vulnerable people.*

As an ombudsman, for example, I spoke to an administrator about an elderly resident ashamed to eat in the dining room, due to her having no teeth. She had no family and needed someone to intervene as her advocate. She was able to get proper-fitting dentures, eat real food in the dining room, and socialize with other residents. "You have the power to make the world better. Try it and see."

John Barnett's words of advice are so powerful. By now, I hope you are inspired to choose to focus your time freedom and ward off boredom and aimlessness. With so much time affluence now, are you willing to use this abundant resource as a valuable tool for Good?

Like gardening or teaching others to garden. Like tutoring children because they are our next generation, says Woody Clinard, my podcast guest and tutor of seventeen years. His first students are graduating now from high school but were at risk of becoming dropouts, which results in being a service worker or on welfare. Invest time, if not in your nuclear family, find one to adopt. David 'Woody' Clinard is rich with memories of making a difference in a stranger's lifetime.

Contentment, wow!

ACTIONS TO TAKE

- Make a list of your skills that are transferable, and can be used in a variety of ways. For example, communication skills can be used verbally, writing and in managing. Analytical and project management are also used in various ways.

- DO WHAT YOU DID FOR CHARITY. This is the quickest way to get involved in something outside of yourself after you retire, thereby saving time until something else intrigues you, advises author/humanitarian Cynthia Kersey.

- Consider the following:

  – Are you in a growth mindset or a decline mindset?

  – What intrigues you about retirement?

  – How could you become as curious as a three-year-old?

Counterintuitive: Purpose gives you MORE time—61 percent fewer nights in the hospital, 31 percent fewer doctor visits, and fewer cases of dementia.

Radiate Possibility

CHAPTER THREE

Building Social Networks

Seniors who socialize are happier. A bold statement but very true.

Carol Penny needed to retire because her husband was starting to develop dementia. She had contributed extensively in the childcare industry; it was a job that fit her like a glove. She loved her husband dearly. Besides, she had grandkids coming along now. So, they would add to feed her spirit during her caregiving days. Then, an amazing thing happened. She noticed how well her grandkids and her husband got along singing, dancing and playing. They were happier together! She then used her ingenuity to create a new business to benefit many others in the same situation. She turned an obstacle into an opportunity—Bridgestogether. org.

Most people miss their social interactions *more* than their paychecks when they retire. Besides coworkers and colleagues being almost like family, they also help us feel valued, challenged, useful and important. In so many ways, our work keeps us mentally healthy and socially healthy. It helps us know ourselves, too.

When you aren't leaving the house on a daily basis, all of those good interactions become absent. So now, does going to the grocery store become your big event? I've seen a couple of cars in the grocery store parking lot with a senior sitting alone in each one, just watching people come and go. It makes me sad that that could be the extent of their social life but glad too that at least they are outside and dressed.

What hobbies do you have that could replace your work family where you perhaps had problems to solve together, challenges to overcome, and felt valuable?

Which events, such as with church or faith-based, book, auto or card clubs keep you socially and mentally healthy?

Who do you laugh with? Celebrate with? Have lunch with?

Volunteering is a great way to enrich you socially and to feel useful and valued. Realize, sooner than later, that isolation is the Enemy. You are responsible for your social life. Isolation results in higher healthcare costs, a shorter life, and leads to feelings of sadness and abandonment that can lead to depression; that could lead to alcoholism and/or suicide.

There is actually a looming isolation crisis on the horizon if we don't address the loneliness issue soon! This is the era when contraceptives and abortion became legal. When so many retirees' activities are centered around the next generation, that's *missing* for nearly one in five retirees. Married or single.

I'm one of these Boomers without kids. I have thirteen nieces and nephews. Though I wanted to contribute to their lives significantly, it turned out that I moved to the other corner of the nation during the time I could have built strong relationships and impacted them the most. So as adults, we don't know each other very well. This challenges my sense of Community a lot. I used to be quite involved with my church's single ministry during my late thirties and forties. Now, there aren't very many of those around anymore.

I'm an introvert so my need to be social is lower, but my need to be socially healthy is the *same* as anyone. So, during the challenges of the pandemic lockdown of 2020, I was active on zoom about three days a week and sometimes three or four events a day. So I felt healthy. And, I'm coming to find now that there are a few new solutions evolving to combat isolation online (WISDO & Talk-Time). There are even cohousing options (see Going Deeper).

I like to use visual aids, like Post-it notes, for important reminders (like healthy snacks). Making a list of a variety of ways to be active socially might help you. Or, making a game of it, like Bingo, to keep dates on your calendar for being social. Choir, orchestra, mentor/tutor, volunteer, church, card game nights, theater, baseball games, hobbies, movies, woodworking, community events, hikes, yoga, garden club, rockhounds, dog walking, etc.

I'm hoping we get back to having more potlucks, sing-alongs etc. I remember a time when I was going through abuse recovery work that I'd purposefully give hugs at church so I could *get* some. I was so hungry and even afraid I'd crumble emotionally into pieces for a bit. Have you been there? Realize, my friend, we all will be single at some point before we die. Where your spouse may be in charge of, or in control of, your social calendar, that can and will change. You are responsible. Put birthdays and anniversaries on your calendar, and hobbies and bridge club too. Get out there—your health and life depend on it.

I remember talking to a coworker when I was in my twenties about having a "grass is greener" sense about life. She traveled a fair amount. I was shocked when she explained her husband preferred being home. What I learned from her was that she didn't let her sense of adventure keep her home, too. Don't let life pass you by. Do it alone if you have to. And I have—like my trip to Italy.

Laughter is better together. Cake and ice cream are better with friends. Hiking is better together. Prayer is better together. Songs are, too.

I wonder if it's possible to equate social activities on our calendars with self-care? With social health? With mental health? With longer life? With less need for medicine?

I wonder if it is possible to equate a walk in the park with combating depression. Having a dog to walk as being the medicine for isolation.

Side Note: A few years back I asked myself a challenging question: "How much do I believe the Bible? 10 percent?, 20 percent?, 70 percent? or 100 percent?" A LOT of the stories are pretty amazing! My answer was probably around 40 to 60 percent at the time. Over time, I recalled my Texas pastor preaching on "nothing is impossible" a few times. Or, "all things are possible." It grew my faith and my belief in what's possible. A LOT. Such a difference, especially since quantum physics is helping us to understand and explain so many things now. So, what would your answer be? You may be at 10 percent: good, you can start from there.

My podcast guest Dr. Sara Geber Zeff is a professional speaker, a certified retirement coach, and a recognized expert in planning the next stage of life to people fifty-plus years in order to better prepare for the future. Her research turned up a big difference in retirement years with whether people had children or not.

When she started to look into how widespread the potential problem is, she discovered that according to a 2010 Pew research study, almost 20 percent of Baby Boomer women did not have children. This research also showed her a big difference in how to look and plan for life without children.

Now, she calls people who are aging without having adult children, as a kind of a safety net, "Solo-Agers." Neither she nor her husband has kids. Noticing this difference, she wondered who's going to respond to any call for help. The answer was nobody, since both their parents had already passed on.

Solo aging is not just people who do not have children, and are aging alone. For various other reasons—some have children but they are living thousands of miles away, or they may be estranged, or there could be all kinds of reasons—some have become Solo-Agers too.

About ten years ago, Sara saw how most of her contemporaries were spending a tremendous amount of time flying all over the country, or were trying to arrange things long distance to take care of their aging parent. Or, spending a lot of time with those parents just doing a whole host of things.

One in five of the Baby Boomer women does not have her own children due to The Pill (birth control), and access to more higher education opportunities. Some may be raising, or may have raised, stepchildren and be close to them, but there really is no actual replacement often for our own children, in terms of helping us as we get older. We will have to come up with our own unique ways to cope or excel by planning ahead so we won't be isolated and lonely in our later years.

How will we fill the need for nurturing relationships throughout our lives, continuing into later in life? This is important for many reasons.

First, adult children often do many things for their aging parents. They are the primary social support system for things like shopping, picking up prescriptions, and going to doctor appointments. It may include management of real estate transactions, if the parents are in a retirement community. It may include taking care of financial obligations, paying the bills, making investment decisions as their parents' cognitive ability decreases. It just becomes very difficult for older ones. Night driving becomes difficult, and as their vision starts to deteriorate even daytime driving doesn't feel particularly safe any longer.

You might ask a niece or a nephew to check in on you at least on a monthly basis, just to see how you're doing. If they notice any changes, call it to someone's attention, and then maybe set up a connection with your primary care physician or your financial advisor or your estate attorney, because these are all services we typically hire to help us out, both while we're in the prime of life and now.

When Sara first started doing this work, she realized her own circle of friends were all her same age. Then through a book group she had joined, she gained many friends in their forties.

As intergenerational friendships grow and we learn more about each other's lives, they will be potential candidates to help with things as you age. Begin the conversations now about how you are concerned about being isolated as an older adult, and start talking to them about how isolation can be prevented and how they could help you.

Consider moving to be closer to family. If you don't have family, consider strongly the potential for joining a senior housing community like a wonderful mobile home park. Mobile home parks are great because they have common areas where everybody picks up their mail and laundry. Find a community where you are expected to interact with others on a regular basis. We need to be aging in a community of some sort where there are lots of different clubs and interest groups to join right there.

The three most important challenges for Solo-Agers are housing, care and social connections. Make plans so that you are attending to these three as best you can. This applies to both parents and Solo-Agers.

Sara encourages Solo-Agers to at least look into long-term care insurance. Think what it might be like to live with some of your friends, either in a large home or in an adjacent apartment, or in a senior community where you can still continue to enjoy each other's company. Home-sharing has become more and more popular for older adults, being able to spend quality time with people you love.

Successful aging is the ability to make changes and be adaptable to the things that happen to us as we get older. Rally around your friends, so they are there when you need them, and perhaps vice-versa.

Social Support Networks are critical to a happy retirement, to our well-being, and to successful aging. Here are some of Sara's tips:

- Understand transportation options

- Get and stay involved

- Get a dog

- Maintain ties to places of worship

- Be flexible—about everything

- Arrange dining with others out or in

- Use adaptive technology

- Stay in touch with neighbors

- Get your hearing and vision checked annually

Sara's website (sarazeffgeber.com) has lots of freebies to help you with your planning, decision-making, leaving a legacy, and completing your personal relationship evaluation worksheet. There's also a worksheet on the criteria for living outside the home, for age-friendly homes, and making our homes safer for older people.

ACTIONS TO TAKE

- Make a list of five current habits that empower you (e.g. 7-8 hours of sleep daily).

- Make a list of five current habits that hold you back or get in your way.

- List five habits you would like to explore or adopt more fully.

- Use your gift of gab to talk to lonely people or kids at compassionate/ buddy benches.

cherish forever
what makes you
unique.

CHAPTER FOUR

Gain Status

Was your job *very* demanding? Very competitive? Required lots of travel and/or overtime?

Walking away from a job that consumed so much of your energy, brain power and focus will likely feel like entering a whole new world overnight when you retire. No stress. No travel. No overtime. No demands. Nothing to solve, to fix or accomplish. Whoosh! Gone. Even your high-tech gadgets are mostly gone. Is your wardrobe completely different, too?

Who are you now that you can sleep all day? Where do you need to be—the coffee shop?!!

Besides this, the U.S. is known as the no-vacation-nation. Workaholics, we are. What in the world are we going to do with free time?

Your job gave you status. A business card and title. Responsibilities – GONE. What's even worse is if you were shown the door by surprise—or a pandemic. Nobody to lead. Nothing to control.

Your life actually had been severely out of balance—maybe for decades. What this means is, you had NO time for friends, clubs, hobbies, spirituality, pleasure and maybe even limited family time. They were nonexistent. Therein is the vacancy, where others would have a support system to draw on once retirement was reached. For you, you no longer know who you are. It's an out-to-pasture feeling.

This identity crisis shows up as questioning your role in society, searching for more meaning, reason or passion for life. You might even be questioning your values, spirituality, beliefs and interests. Transitions are tough; confusion and exhaustion are common. You are in a different place in your life.

Stop. Comparisons mean trouble. Internal and external judgment solves nothing. Find support through the people surrounding you. They help us know who we are—like mirrors. Focus on your greatness—it just needs a NEW landing place!

Acknowledge your transition. It strengthens your self-image and starts to restore your confidence. A renewed sense of self and your contribution to society helps you to see yourself as acceptable and starts the healing process. It's a pivotal time. Tell yourself, "I don't know all the answers yet and that's just fine!"

I wonder if taking a year off, like college grads sometimes do to find themselves, would be a good idea. To consider your possibilities. To find your heart again. To listen deeply. To find where you left your joy. To get life back in balance. To find a new rhythm to life now.

The simplest and perhaps easiest transition is to go with this solution: Do what you did, only do it for charity. Accountant—find a foundation that needs a bean counter. Pilot—find a mission needing people or things delivered.

This is where I like to use a question from *The Lion King*: Have you forgotten who you are? You are still the college graduate. You are still the giant of a person with a gentle heart. You are still a person of strong character, responsibility and leadership skills. People can still count on you. This hasn't changed! Just a little lifestyle rebalancing is needed to get you back on level ground and sure footing.

Fight the temptation to disappear into alcoholism. Or, endless TV or internet. (Or any addiction) You will be making room for depression, a lower quality of life, misery, and higher healthcare costs. This is so important; I challenge you to have a friend or colleague hold you accountable and check on you weekly. Or, whatever it takes.

I was surprised when I learned from a young podcast guest that there are two kinds of fun: one is solitary and one is social. Did you realize enjoying your own company is important? I wonder if it's possible to reacquaint yourself with where your fun and pleasure come from. What touches your heart? What's satisfying to you?

A big transition for me came when I accepted a job transfer to Tampa, Florida. A friend made a video at my goodbye party of "words of wisdom" from my parting friends. The best nugget in that video was "Give yourself at *least* six months to adjust and find or make a new circle of friends!" At three months, I thought I was good, but at five months, it felt like I'd hit a brick wall! So, reminding myself of their wise words helped me hang on a little longer.

Remember, you are more than your job. It's important to embrace and derive value from other roles in your life: son/daughter, brother/sister, spouse/partner, father/mother. The ability to detach emotionally from your work can make you better at living.

I wonder if it's possible for you to find a need in your community, church or family that needs attention. What project could you take on that could make a difference to someone? And, at the same time, engaging your heartstrings can actually save you, too. What legacy could make you come alive, be worth your full energy, and start you working in the direction of a new future?

The need I found in my community was at the senior center. They told me they were combating isolation and depression. Since so many Boomers are retiring or will soon, I created a workshop and collected lots of resource ideas to help them expand "what's possible" for them. Movies, books, and websites. Even used my fabric art blocks to inspire ideas in my *What Do I Want to Do in Retirement?* workshop. The seniors' comments at the end of class that I gave them lots to think about were very satisfying for me!

Then, after being invited to be a guest on a talk show, I started wondering if it was possible to be more of an influencer? I started being curious and courageous in the new adventure of learning to be a podcaster and to inspire others on a larger scale. The challenge, however, was that podcasts weren't yet popular with the Boomers. I'd have to build an audience, too. Yet, I saw it as planting seeds. Now, I have a bigger field in which to sow seeds—through writing.

You *are* still worthwhile and have so much talent and experience. What was it about your career in the beginning that was fully engaging? What were you passionate about? Who needs what you know and wants to learn, be mentored and developed? Someone else needs saving, too!

My podcast guest, the late esteemed Professor Emeritus Frank Caro, was amazing. After retiring from the University of Massachusetts Boston, he remained active in research and community service through volunteerism. He spearheaded and directed accomplishments that improved the quality of life, not only for older adults, but for residents of all ages in his community of Brookline, a suburb of Boston. He actually cofounded the Brookline Community Aging Network and it is part of the Massachusetts healthy aging collaborative, with a mission to make a city a better place to grow old. He led the Brookline community into the World Health Organization's Age-Friendly Community program, and was very active in Town Meetings for sixteen years.

Frank's personal time and joy seemed to have no limits, ranging from gardening to home brewing to pottery-making.

Here is a portion of my interview.

"I like to grow all kinds of things. I'm currently concentrating on house plants. I do what can be called functional pottery that are useful things for the household, emphasizing useful things for food service and planters. I've become known for my French butter dishes."

Question: What conditions do you care about? Or monitor and report, like what conditions are you an advocate for in your community? Is your community a good place for older people to live?

"We call attention to the good things that this community offers. And we nudge a little bit, to try to make things better.

"One of the things that we started with was a concern from one of our members about restrooms that were available to the public. Then, let's make that information widely available on our website.

"Another thing we are concerned about is the condition of sidewalks after a winter storm. We live in a community that is basically very walkable, and we have a lot of people, including a lot of older people who like to get out after snowstorms and go about their affairs. And one of the issues is if the sidewalks are clear, is it safe for people to get out on the sidewalks? We set up a winter sidewalk monitoring team. The town did a considerable amount of public education on the need to keep the sidewalks clear. And we've had substantial improvements in the condition of sidewalks after storms. This is something that benefits people of all ages.

"We've made a list of elevators that are both residential buildings and automatic door openers in business buildings. Now people in wheelchairs can know that they can get around and see the various business and government kinds of offices, because there are elevators available to reach them.

"I think it's simple things that don't take an engineer to change. It just takes being our brother's keeper and helping people to know what works for them in their community. And we want to engage them. The productive aging moments take a kind of an opposite perspective where the kind of notion is that older people find it most meaningful to continue to be active throughout their lives. Remain engaged. Political life. Artistic expression.

"The response in Canada has been particularly strong. And here, the first major cities to get started were Portland, Oregon; New York City, Chicago, and Philly. But it's something that the police department, the fire department, the health department, public works department, parks department—*everybody* is involved in. So that makes it really much stronger than just an advocacy effort of a small number of mostly older people. It encourages communities to be sensitive to the needs of people of all ages.

"Think of the timing of traffic lights: if you have some people who take twenty seconds to cross the street, how are you going to help them? And wait, we really need to make our communities livable for everybody.

"There's kind of two ways to approach this whole process. One is through assessment of needs and then doing planning and taking action.

"You could take what your strengths are and what could be improved and address it that way. Portland, Oregon, is a municipality that is really exemplary in the way in which it took up the planful approach. When it joined the Age-Friendly City Initiative, it teamed up with a group that was associated with Portland State University and a group involving some older people there. And they did a very systematic study of the community needs before they committed themselves to taking any action. So, they really wanted to understand the demographics, the number of older people, the characteristics of the older people. And they took kind of a very systematic multiyear effort in planning to address it.

"One of the things that we did was we set up an age-friendly TV show that is operated through our public access television station. We have a group that puts on that show. They put on a new show every six weeks or so.

"We figured we can find people as we go along to enable us to make some things happen. We were very much focused on what it's possible to do with modest resources. Then, advertise our needs on the website. We are doing a mix of things, but we're very pragmatic about the way we approach things. We're very aware of what can be done very simply at little or no cost.

"Now it's becoming known as the village movement. That's really older people getting together to talk about what can be done to enable them to continue to live successfully in their homes or communities. And, in our case, we were fortunate to have a senior center director who wanted to be part of that discussion. More can be accomplished if people work in groups than if they work individually."

Frank Caro's legacy in the field of gerontology was truly remarkable.

Let's accept this time of your life as a temporary short-lived time of confusion into retirement—a seasonal change. Your sights are on gaining new insight into who you've become over the recent decades to bring you to this new destination. You are taking a deep, slow, long breath in of FRESH COURAGE. The confusion will soon be behind you as you focus on your inner wisdom and self-discovery. Your old clothes don't fit any longer and you are looking for a new wardrobe. That's a good thing because you aim to align the person you've become with your new Essence and new choices. You intend to leave a powerful legacy, find a new joy in exploring the future, and to live a meaningful life. Fulfillment will extend your longevity and reap deep satisfaction.

ACTIONS TO TAKE

- List twenty things you love to do.

- List five desires, wishes or goals in EACH of these key areas of life:
  - Self
  - Relationships
  - Creativity
  - Helpful People/Support
  - Career
  - Wisdom/Self-Knowledge
  - Family
  - Wealth/Prosperity
  - Fame/Reputation

- How long has it been since you said THANK YOU?

- How long has it been since you said "What do you think?

- Become a wisdom well—a source of help where others come to replenish their courage, understand life twists and turns, generate curiosity and resilience.

Explore the
possibilities

CHAPTER FIVE

Accumulate Resources

What is your perspective on life: scarcity or abundance? When is enough, enough?

My situation now may not be that much different than yours. My savings will likely last me past the age of ninety, but there's not a lot of room for extras or surprises, like trips and special events. The need for new things isn't the same in this season of life. Besides, I get a kick out of finding second-hand things that "do the job" when I am in need of something. My focus now is on maintaining the house and car and keeping the bills paid.

For me, accumulating resources means something different now. And, for you, it's more likely focused on things outside of yourself and your household. But we want more than survival; let's thrive, right? The survive-and-thrive issue now includes your kids and grandkids. Spending our discretionary income often is for others! Traveling to their special events. Helping them get clothes for school or books, or a new lawn mower. Right?

An amazing book I read was *The Soul of Money*, by Lynne Twist, a global activist and consummate fundraiser. What took me by surprise was that I didn't learn what I thought I would when I read it. The author has worked with people who are ultra-billionaires as well as people whose lives didn't include any money. The full spectrum! You might have heard it said some of the happiest people are poor. But she found their living without money made them rich in other ways. Lots of other ways. The lesson I came away with was, it's what's in our heart that gives money meaning and value.

Another book, *Love Money, Money Loves You*, described money as energy or a motivator. You know, like when you're a teenager and you want a car? You figure out a way to get a job so you can buy a car. The need you felt motivated you (energized you) to find a solution—trade work hours for a paycheck to get a car. My sister had an accident at her first job and she spent the insurance settlement to buy her first car. A car needs to be insured, however. So, the need for insurance (money) motivated her to return to work!

If you worry a lot, you might have a scarcity mindset badgering you about how will you ever pay for a new water heater or a trip plus a gift to attend your grandson's wedding next summer two states away. Some of those worries include the fear of not having what it takes with your fixed income. Add to that a low self-confidence and you just can't figure out what to do. However, should someone ask you about this blessed event and how it's going to work out for you, admitting you might need help is hard to do, so you say, "I've got enough." Then worry some more! What a problem!

So when we have a mindset that "things will work out," we intend to survive and thrive. Whew! What a relief. We can stand taller, lift our chin, find some curiosity, and be open to possibilities. Opportunities may turn up to walk your neighbor's dog for a couple of weeks, or house sit for someone. Then, you get to anticipate the trip! Do you feel poor, now?

Let's say, accumulating resources from a perspective of abundance allows you the pleasure of helping a few people to have a better life. Their job and success then can be enjoyed by you, too. Double win!

Entertaining possibilities on a regular basis invites an element of faith, courage, curiosity and risk. It may require being vulnerable, too. And *that's* when creativity is born. *Until* you are willing to *see* if something good could turn up in your favor, you can't and won't see an opportunity when it appears.

The cultures where money is absent is where value is expressed and experienced in many *other* ways. Taking care of each other is very common. Perhaps it's like having all things in common—you need it, it's yours. Tending food and crops is done together. Raising families is a community event. Wisdom is collectively used when decisions need to be made.

Would you be willing to consider what other resources you have besides money today? Assets, belongings, supplies and support? How about voice, smell, touch, sight and taste? How about a warm heart, fortitude, love, skills, abilities and wisdom? What about the people you know and your education, knowledge, beliefs and experiences? WOW! It's impressive! With all these resources, what isn't possible? You are enough. You *have* enough.

Remember, risk and a leap of faith could make the difference. In fact, it could even be energizing. So, even though I haven't an abundance of money as yet, it didn't stop me from making fifty-three podcasts. And, I created and taught thirty workshops at my area senior centers. I also contributed a dozen articles for my local paper. Then, in the future, with FRESH COURAGE, I anticipate funding college scholarships for young women.

To all these resources that you have, let's add the element of what matters to you: your values. It's a subject rarely discussed. How you use money speaks a lot about what matters to you. What other resources?

Clarifying your values can be a real eye-opener. Then reflect on how your current choices line up with your values. Significant question: What story does your checkbook tell about your values? Until they align, you may find yourself in many frustrating situations. And you've wondered why, right? Life is good, when you honor and live your values; the things that really matter to you.

You are a valuable nugget of accumulated resources! Engage your natural resources now to shine. It's your time to shine! Success is now about making a difference from your heart, experience, talents and accumulated knowledge! In retirement, you have the freedom to be your own boss like never before perhaps, and the drive to survive and thrive. Being socially and emotionally healthy, helping others to have a better life also matters to you because life is better together. Your clarified values will help you sift through the opportunities that show up in order to know where there will be a fit.

So let's look beyond accumulating more things. Let's accumulate more friends and experiences and continue to grow. Volunteering is a great way to do this. Trade in monotonous, boring days for things that energize you.

Then you won't be home should sadness and depression come knocking at your door.

The values clarification process is powerful because it helps you understand why certain things bother you, such as stories in the news. Once you know what's important to you, you can stand for something and pursue something with conviction. It could turn out to be your *purpose.* How satisfying would that be!

My podcast guest this time, motivational speaker Paul Long, takes the 'excuse mindset' approach: why change now? If our careers became monotonous, retirement may provoke a "who needs me now?" attitude and our excuses turn us into sadness, despair and depression, which may precede dementia, alcoholism or suicide.

Paul posed a question for our audience: "Imagine going back into your twenties, when you're looking at your life and your career ahead of you and trying to figure out 'what do I want to do with my life?' Well, back then, you didn't know much. You didn't know much about yourself and you didn't know much about life.

"Now, imagine this time in your life as being in that place again, except you *do* know yourself, you *do* know what you like and what you *don't* like, and what you're good at and what you're not good at. Now is an opportunity to do something that you want to do, and it doesn't have to be forty or eighty hours a week."

What could be your excuse for not moving forward or for not taking a bit of a risk or trying something new? When I say risk, I don't necessarily mean financial risk. There are all the *internal* so-called risks that we have. But I also thought about the rocking chair test—that the Number One regret people have is that they didn't go forward. They didn't go for something.

I then posed the question to several professionals: What are the common excuses for not moving forward, not taking a risk and trying something new, and how can we overcome it?

Excuse #1: *I'm not creative. I'm not a big idea person, I don't have anything interesting.*

Author Tim Ferriss says to ask yourself, "What excites me?" "What do I love?"

Consultant Alaina Love created a Passion Profiler: https://thepurposelink.com/passion-profiler/ to help you discover the core passions you need to address to have a fulfilling life.

Author Jay Samit suggests putting a tablet next to your toothbrush or your bed. And every day before you go to bed, write down three problems you saw or experienced that day. What happens over that 30 days is you've not only come up with an impressive list, but all of a sudden there are certain problems and needs that you're seeing that start resonating within you. In fact, I'll lay you high odds that some of those ideas, if not one of those ideas, all of a sudden, you're going to find yourself thinking about it. It's going to be percolating organically within your mind. And you're going to identify it because you can relate to it and you can have an idea for it.

Then look at your skills, look at your talents, look at your abilities and start applying those. Google it called: how entrepreneurs come up with great ideas.

Excuse #2: *I'm too old.*

Considering the fact you've got all these years of healthy life ahead of you, you aren't too old. Be present in life. Be grounded and observe things. Ideas are abundant; drive isn't. I have three feet of file drawers behind my desk full of great ideas that never came to fruition because I didn't have the drive do anything with them. Right.

Let your subconscious do the work here again. When you start thinking and seeing all these problems, your subconscious will start taking over to attack practical problems. Head into the weird places. Think out of the box and think out of the box about yourself. We are all more capable and have more options than we ever imagined. We're the most self-limiting creatures on the planet. Search for a better way. Think big.

Get inspired by history. I could give you example after example of people who were like, who the heck am I to do this? Who did it? And they're famous and they succeeded. They made a difference in our world. Also be inspired by what is happening now. More and more people over fifty are reimaging and reinventing by starting businesses, pivoting careers, becoming professional gig workers (contractors), and the list goes on. It is a mega trend you can join.

Be prepared to shift gears, whatever you're imagining. Now it's going to be different. It may take longer; six months from now or six years from now. You can't rush the brain to overcome Excuse Number Two about not having the right skills or experience or knowledge. And if you really stop for a moment and think about it, in the first place, in this day and age, are you kidding me? When anyone can go on Google or YouTube to learn *anything*, you can discover any skill or experience or knowledge you need to know, now.

Excuse #3: *I don't have time.*

We're always seeming to talk about not having enough time. And, by the way, besides ProBoomer, I still have my content creation business going, plus I'm in a multi-decade relationship. I have two sons. Granted, they've moved away, but I never stop being a parent. I heard somebody put it this way: Whether you're rich or poor; whether you're famous, successful, or whatever, you only have twenty-four hours in a day. We all only have twenty-four hours in a day.

In my case, every morning when I do yoga, I listen to these people on YouTube. It's absolutely amazing. YouTube is one of the most phenomenal tools ever. And I listen to people like Tim Ferriss or John Assaraf, or James Clear, who's a habit hacker. Brian Tracy and Brendan Bouchard, who have these methods that you don't have to necessarily embrace. This goes way beyond the Stephen Covey planners, but ways to be more efficient with your time; ways to be more effective in focus.

It's having the habits to get up and go and do things. I love what James Clear says, because when you do have a busy life and you're trying to just start something that you don't necessarily have a boss or a loved one demanding it of you, it's hard to get it done. Clear says focus not on the whole goal or task, just focus on the first one percent. Want to get in shape? Just focus on getting your workout shoes on and take it from there. You get in that habit and it works.

The point is that we *do* have time. As we're getting older, we are hearing the clock tick and we do still have our whole lives in front of us, but we do have more limited time, even if it is thirty or forty or fifty years. So that's the other side of the coin. We've got more time than we think we do. And in some ways, it's almost more important now for us to find things that give us relevance and purpose and to make a difference.

Now you have to set your own deadlines. It really is about personal performance. Set deadlines for yourself. When are you going to get this part figured out? When are you going to figure that out? You make time for the priorities because it's personal.

Excuse #4: *I'm too late.*

Or, I'm too late in life. Actually, the opposite is true. This is probably the most optimum time of existence in human history, as well as in your life, when you've got the experience, the knowledge, the skills you've honed. How many people flourish? Monet did his greatest paintings in his eighties when he said, "I think I finally got it figured out!"

You've got the networks of friends, family and colleagues. You've got the money. You don't always need to invent something new, but look at applications and technology or solutions or businesses and everything, and you can have a better way of doing it. Or you can have a way that's more suitable for your target audience.

For example, consider this: Getting older. Okay. At some point in our lives, you know, even though we've been talking about how healthy and vibrant and all the possibilities we have into our seventies, eighties, and even nineties, there is probably going to come a time when we are more challenged, aka assisted living, where we really need some care that needs reinventing.

The current situation in every way, shape or form does not cut it. If you've had older parents or you know other people who have gone through it, you know what a nightmare it can be and how inappropriate it is. There are some people that are in Aging 2.0. Look it up online, people trying to do it better. So who better than us, because we're taking care of ourselves in our own future. That's something that could be transformed.

Excuse #5: *I can't take the risk and especially who am I to do this?*

There are now millions of different iterations of how people were continuing to work into older age, from being a consultant to part-time, special projects, to whatever. Two quotes to remember, the first one from Mark Twain — Twenty years from now, you will be more disappointed by the things you didn't do than by the ones you did explore, dream, discover. The second from Helen Keller — Security is mostly a superstition. Life is either a daring adventure or nothing.

What I'm really going to regret is not going after it; not my legacy. Yes. I had great careers. Yes, I raised two wonderful children. I had a phenomenal relationship, but I mean, really, you know, what am I going to regret? Not going after it. And, so I've literally envisioned how I would feel if I didn't go after my ProBoomer/New Way Forward idea. Even though I've got challenges, even though it's a lot of hours and everything it is so fulfilling to do this. It is literally a journey I am enjoying.

I'll interject something here: Paul made an award-winning documentary about how the Peace Corps and the "'60s" got started. I think this is an ideal time for us Boomers to get reengaged with the Peace Corps. It's one hour long and marked the 50th anniversary of presidential candidate John F. Kennedy on the campus of the University of Michigan, giving an impromptu speech to 10,000 students and bringing up the concept of the Peace Corps. That was the first time in history, the youth—the Baby Boomers—were able to say, wait a minute, I'm not going to live my life the way my parents or society expects me to; we're going to do things differently. I really enjoyed it and remember it being covered on the news then. I recommend watching *A Passing of the Torch* on https://vimeo.com/73799145

ACTIONS TO TAKE

- Clarify your values because values are the principles and standards guiding your decisions and behavior. They help us walk our talk. So get clear on what *truly matters* to you. Here's a great list; circle a dozen or so that are important, then narrow the list down by prioritizing the top half, then reduce it half again. This list is from Dr. Brené Brown's website: https://daretolead.brenebrown.com/wp-content/uploads/2019/02/Values.pdf

- List four peak experiences that made you feel really terrific, such as winning a marathon, earning a degree, or the birth of a child, etc. Then, what was it about them that made you feel so terrific—fulfillment, satisfaction, happiness—being as specific as possible.

- List four of your 'hot buttons'…situations or attitudes that really aggravate you, such as, entitlement, rudeness, ringing phones in meetings, etc. Then, what is it *about* the hot buttons that aggravates you?—selfishness, disrespect, etc.

Based on your review of the above, what would you say are your four CORE VALUES that are most important to you in your life right now?

Everyone has a seed
of greatness
buried in a gift
needed by the world.

- Myles Munroe

CHAPTER SIX

Be Generous

Generosity comes in many forms. Whether you are just starting out as a giver or are a regular, serious giver, giving is one of the best ways to "pay it forward." It is meaningful in large, overt ways or in little ways. If you think of your generosity like vanilla extract in baking, a little bit goes a long way. Never underestimate the value others will find from your giving.

What makes you feel alive? What makes your heart sing?

Longtime philanthropist and visionary Lynne Twist says sharing makes everything better. Sharing frees up an *"ocean of energy."* And, it frees us from the chase and myth of "more is better." Pay attention to what you already have. When you appreciate what you have been given, *it appreciates.* You can celebrate what you accomplish. In this, we find a sufficiency that's *fulfilling.*

In *What Retirees Want: A Holistic View of Life's Third Age*, Dr. Ken Dychtwald and author Robert Morison's research found today's retirees want to be useful. What helps is having a strong sense of purpose that results in being more active, healthier, happier and feeling young. In our younger years, raising a family and our jobs were central to connecting us to purpose. But purpose can be largely internal, rooted in self-knowledge, self-improvement, and self-actualization.

This fits for me because I always liked to learn. I wasn't driven by it, like being a perpetual student, but I remember distinctly moving forward in some recovery work because it would enable me to help the people coming behind me. It felt like my learning and transformation were maybe for the greater good in some way.

Purpose can also be largely external and social, being focused on success, goals or contributing to the welfare of others. And, purpose can be spiritually based where it combines the inner and external.

Looking back on your journey to this point, where did you get your sense of purpose? Was it in your accomplishments? What do you accomplish now?

Months will turn into years before you know it. Sadness often turns into despair and powerlessness; anger turns into distance and then into withdrawal. Letdown brings on betrayal; depression turns into emptiness. No doubt you yearn to make a difference and fit in somewhere, again.

Let's sidestep any frustration by making a plan.

In what way could you see yourself finding purpose going forward from where you are right now? Since the future is all yours to choose, what appeals to you? Being generous takes on many forms: time, talent and treasure. Reading to someone, being a book lender, listening, running errands for a neighbor, or donating a dollar a day to a charity.

Always being solo, leaving a legacy seemed mostly irrelevant to me. I thought about it a little when I made up my will, but it was nothing earth-shaking. More like 'oh, well!' But now, that's changing. As I am becoming more courageous and my dreams are getting bigger, I'm getting more of an idea of how and why I can contribute, from my unique DNA and my growing interest in being influential for good. Now I aspire to provide college scholarships for young women; that feels quite fulfilling. And, more recently, to love more deeply and impact more broadly. Growth and transformation!

So perhaps your purpose will show up "in time" or as you continue to grow. You could have more resources than I and already have had more opportunities and more connections. Your expertise might exactly fit the need of a foundation or charity. Perhaps with your marketing and social media savvy your creativity knows how to help agencies to grow and expand. You have a glimpse of where you could fit in and make a difference; a purpose and legacy you would love.

It's possible to imagine that most of us want to help others (like grandparents with grandkids) have a better life. Influence, mentor, support or share your experiences and wisdom. Could be that there are kids in your neighborhood, kids of your friends, or nieces and nephews who need your help. Do you doubt you could? Does it seem like a mystery to you? How? Where? Don't have a clue? Be willing to trust the process—the mystery of life.

Yet, there could be something tugging at you in the back corners of your mind and heart that you need to make up for some mistake you made in the past. Or, you want to help others *not* make the same mistakes you made? You've got a hunch how you transformed a failure into a learning experience. *That* could be a goldmine for someone else!

I want to impress upon you that the reward of investing your experiential resources and discretionary time is indeed valuable. Just as the love and understanding you received from others, such as your grandma and grandpa, over the years helped mature you, you can be that same source of inspiration for anyone, my friend. A lot of people need you to help the people coming behind you. I'm amazed at what *isn't* being taught now in our schools, so young people need us to share and mentor or tutor them. (cooking, sewing, canning, for example).

What really anchors their learning experience is for us to share stories and lessons learned along with the skills—the judgment, the reasoning we used, and how it worked out. What we felt and why we did the things we did. There's so much more caught than that which is taught, and is understood with our hearts!

As I became aware of the lack of the emotional planning aspect of retirement, and especially as a behavioral scientist, I was gripped with the travesty of this need. Retirees floundering for two to five years waiting for the Aladdin's Lamp to grant their wish for a purpose is *not* effective. And, it's *not* your fault.

A colleague friend told me of three awesome professional people she knew who died shortly after retiring. I've heard first responders and airline pilots say they have a fear or dread of retiring because their jobs are so demanding that it will leave their lives out-of-balance, and, they also dread leaving their compadres behind.

You may have heard the myth that often people die within three years of retiring. That's just not right, in my mind! I wonder if it is possible for you to embrace curiosity and courage to transform your life: avoid the lost feeling, the frustration of not knowing where you fit in (who are your compadres now?), and uncover what makes your heart sing.

My experience after retiring and figuring out all the paperwork was wondering *how* I would feel productive on a daily basis. Then I remembered a tool we created in my coaching course—an Essence statement.

Tools are good. So, I read mine daily. Sometimes two or three times a day. In fact, I made it into a wall hanging. Gradually, I felt when I lived from my Essence that *every* day felt productive. I was living from my core; what was important to me! Wow! What a great feeling! Each day I was giving my best. It was a sense of alignment with my DNA. Perhaps you would think of it as a convergence zone, too; the ultimate state of feeling alive.

Science now connects happiness with keeping your immunity strong and positive vibrations. It's living my truth and ultimate greatness.

I named my business Effortless Vitality because when you live from your heart, vitality and energy naturally flow effortlessly. Like love. Caring. It's easy. It's expanding. No strain or exertion. No struggle or toil. No pain.

What has given *you* the most joy and success? I'm going to bet it involved others! You made a difference! You changed your corner of the world.

We express what's in our heart and soul with our generosity. Have you ever thought about what money means to you? How do you express your generosity? I have a couple of new friends who teach that money isn't emotional. (It doesn't spend itself, after all!) What you do with what you have expresses what's in your heart. Explore what your generosity means to you.

I also realized that living from my heart aligned me with the principles in *The Secret*, the *Law of Attraction*, and *The Greatest Secret*. I heard writer Rhonda Byrne say, "The more effortless you are, the greater you manifest everything you ever dreamed of."

Psychologist Abraham Maslow would call it self-actualization. Today, it describes the synchronicities or strange and meaningful coincidences; the *inner wisdom* that leads me effortlessly in the path I need to take today.

Something's changed. Your daily addiction, golf games, distractions, alcohol, are losing their hold and you are becoming intrigued with finding your purpose. Acknowledging what bounty you already have and being curious and willing to change your corner of the world sounds like the road to happiness and contentment. With your focused commitment, heart and empowering dreams, let's prove it's your time to shine! I'll be your guide and partner with you to uncover your place to thrive.

I've had a visual aspiration to see billboards around the country with messages beckoning Boomers in retirement to lend their know-how and experience to their favorite charity or foundation.

Or, foundations beckoning the brain and brawn of Boomers to lend a hand.

I wanted to cover this topic in my podcasts but guest speakers couldn't be found. I'd heard of so many professional athletes starting foundations. Why not Boomers? Then I recalled how I was so touched with a story told in *Compassionate Capitalism: Journey to the Soul of Business,* by Blaine Bartlett and David Meltzer. Lee Steinberg, as a sports agent, *required* his clients to give to a socially responsible or social cause that was meaningful to them. This didn't deter athletes from engaging his services, but caused a logjam of athletes having to *wait* for his services. AMAZING! Being required to do good was *attracting* clients!

Maybe this would be where I could find a guest to speak about foundations. So, I got courageous enough to call Blaine and ask. I can still remember where I was when he answered the phone and agreed to schedule a time to be my guest. Then, it turned out that his wife, Cynthia Kersey, who had started her own foundation, was available the day we recorded! Whoa. It was shocking and a delight for me. Kinda left me speechless!

Blaine shared that it was Lee's belief that if these athletes are not willing to give back early and have it as a fundamental part of their career, then there's going to be a very short lifespan in their career. This became a model for the movie *Jerry Maguire*.

Giving is an outlet and it's a creative energy outflow. It is literally the law of abundance—a center of distribution and the cycle of life. Without it, things begin to take a dark turn and become a problem, with accumulation rather than circulation.

In our podcast, Blaine said, "as adults we begin to put clamps on our imagination. Yet imagination is where spirit gets to shine. I don't begin to imagine possibilities until I unleash the spirit. Spirit is where the desire for growth lives. Change and possibility lie in being curious."

In Cynthia's book *Unstoppable* many of the stories show change and possibility coming from being curious. People weren't willing to settle for *not* having the possibilities happen. They were able to give students access to clean water, healthcare, sanitation, healthy food, and training for the parents to generate an income. Then start schools for tourism, agriculture, clinical medicine, nursing and mechanics. Consider a gift to: https://unstoppablefoundation.org/

Blaine added: "Everyone wants to make a difference. There's no other way in retirement of living a life of greater passion, purpose and meaning, and giving leads to health, vitality and wellness. Wherever you are in life, if you're still breathing, you can make a difference. No matter where you are, your life matters."

Now, still breathing, is why Michael Reagan does what he does. He had a job he loved as an artist for the University of Washington for thirty-one years. He had used his artwork to raise millions of dollars for charities, but felt he still needed to do something else to complete himself.

You see, he was a Marine combat veteran in Vietnam in 1967 and '68, and when he came back to the States after serving, some of the drawings of fellow-soldiers he had done over there were *the only pieces* of some of his friends that actually came home.

"I knew I wanted to do something and repay my debt, because I was able to come home alive. The first time you sit in an audience and you see a piece of your art sell for five or six thousand dollars to benefit humanity, it's a life-changing experience. This actually led me to the Fallen Heroes Project."

One of the fallen heroes was Vincent Santaniello (Saint) from Queens, New York, who was Michael's company driver in Vietnam. On March 28, 1968, after being attacked, first with "incoming" rockets, Vinnie died in Mike's arms as he and his Corpsmen Nunn and Milazzo tried to keep him alive. Vinny's last words were, "Mike, I just want to go home." Mike thinks about that moment when Vinny left every single day.

In 2014, Vinny's family flew out to Seattle so Mike could present to them his Fallen Hero portrait of Vinny. And they all agreed, "Vincent's trip home begins right now."

Mike made an original for himself, too. Since then, over more than seventeen years he has poured his heart, soul and incredible gift into every fallen hero drawing he's done—now more than 5,700 free fallen portraits from the U.S., Canada, Poland and Great Britain.

"I care about these people, and because of their sacrifice, it makes me and my art possible.

"I do a portrait in such a way that I believe it includes a personal message. The interesting part about that is, I believe that message, whatever it is, the family is supposed to get. I don't know what that message is but the portraits in many cases carry it home to their family."

His Gold Star families write to him to share some of those messages. Have any of you or your family members been recipients of the Fallen Hero Project?"

Adds Michael: "There's something that drives me to do two portraits every day of soldiers who've died in this war, including suicides of those that served in this war. What I do for twelve hours a day: I look into and draw the face of a Fallen Hero, trying to bring some life back to their family, in a spiritual way. When I do this work, what I'm hoping for is some type of relief for the family, who are going through so much pain.

"With this project, I hear all the stories. I see all the pictures. I get to know the people I'm working with. I study them, I read their diaries. I watched their videos. I talk to their family members before I do their art. I don't sit down and just draw a picture. I learn pretty much all there is to know about them. Because of the spiritual component to this project, it's possible. There's a lot of tears in my house. A lot of energy. I walk miles after I've finished drawing for the day, hoping I can heal my heart a little, because tomorrow I'm going to break it again."

On March 25, 2015, Mike was presented the 2015 Citizen Service Before Self Honor by the Congressional Medal of Honor Society, at Arlington National Cemetery. It is called the Civilian Medal of Honor. The other Medal of Honor recipients present told him, "You're helping all these families heal; all these families that are in horrible pain. You're helping them start living again and you're doing it for free. And you're doing it every day. We wanted to recognize that."

A friend then connected Mike with an attorney to set up a 501(c)3 nonprofit foundation, which means all monetary donations are tax deductible. (The Michael G. Reagan Portrait Foundation.)

The website is fallenheroesproject.org. All of the folks involved in the foundation work for free, including the artist, but like with everything there are still costs involved with distributing these free portraits across the country and to our Allies around the world. There are supplies, office expenses, storage, etc., and mailing costs. Michael does most of the framing work with Hobby Lobby in nearby Lynnwood, Washington. His art website: http://www.michaelgreaganartist.com/. There are also many videos on YouTube about his Fallen Heroes work.

ACTIONS TO TAKE

- Make a list of three things daily you are grateful for.
- Be as curious as you are wise.
- What have you let go of to get you to this place?
- List three to five of your most important guiding principles.

Everyone has guiding principles, mottoes that guide day-to-day living and working. Examples: Trust the process or 'Just do it'.

- What about your life isn't working for you now? What is it costing you?

- If you really like an organization and the cause it serves, get curious about how the operations work. You may find a new passion to work with or gain a better understanding of how contributions are used.

- Assuming the world is perfect right now, what would it look like? What does it feel like?

- If being generous is something you value, do you wish you had more to give?

MASTER YOUR MONEY NOW is the website of my friend Melissa Ternes. She has a FINANCIAL POWER CHECKLIST to download for free to evaluate the health of your wealth at melissaternes.com

May You feed
a hungry world
through me.

CHAPTER SEVEN

Desire Meaning

Are you finding a new sense of Fresh Courage now? I hope so. Something has changed for you. Once you thought you wanted endless pleasure, no demands on your time; to come and go as you please.

But your focus has begun to change. You've become curious and maybe ready to dance with life again. Possibilities that you've never imagined have opened your eyes and heart a bit. It feels good, scary and amazing, too. There's a destiny starting to break through into your imagination. Has it awakened an early dream in you?

The freedom to golf, travel, gamble, dance, hike, sing, play poker, watch videos, be a foodie 365 days a year, isn't holding the same fascination that it used to. The real freedom is having a choice.

Maybe these things have become a distraction or the best choice at the time. Then they became a habit. Or, became your social life.

With new possibilities come new choices. So many things in life take courage. Especially new things. It's looking at where you are and the future, and asking yourself, "Which would I rather have? Grow or stay the same?" The reality though is, grow or become irrelevant and stagnate, then die.

You picked up this book for the hope of something new to grab your attention and focus. Distractions weren't doing it for you anymore. Facebook. Computer or video games. Isolation became toxic.

Maybe you've gotten to the place of being frustrated. You've had better days. You've got more to give or do. You feel it inside. But nobody showed you a plan. Until now.

I'm frustrated too, because this is something everybody needs to know. Dare I say, *wants* to know? Nothing about values gets covered in school or college, unless by a lucky choice of instructors. Then, taking it a step further, to correlate your DNA and values? Nope. Doesn't happen.

Could it be that's why so many people are acting out, frustrated, bitter, or don't feel heard or seen or visible?

Curious people. Resentful people. Welcome to a new day.

I was surprised when my Taylor Protocol profile called me an influencer. Who, *me*? I did agree with "comprehend and express" because that's what I do with my fabric art blocks, where I turn wisdom nuggets from the books I read into pretty wall hangings.

"Influence behavior?" Well, I am a behavioral scientist, but not quite sure about this. Then, "experience the ideal." YES!!! That's why I'm talking to you! The *ideal* of being in love with life, of being fulfilled, of connecting with *your* purpose, not just *a* purpose. Heaven on earth! Being true to your heart.

When you feel your life flowing effortlessly from your heart through your purpose, it feels like you are in love with life. Alive. Like heaven on earth. What could be better than this? Delightful.

Yet, writing my first book took lots of courage. It's like putting on a new garment to see how it fits. Having and knowing your Essence gives you a new confidence that, in time, it'll be the right choice. At first, you may even have to grow into it. *I* did. I had to dig deep, pulling things from deep inside myself to share with you and make it my best.

Like you, I want a cause to champion. When I considered retirement, I didn't have any great examples. My mom was a stay-at-homemaker. My older brother and sister didn't see retirement due to fatal accidents. And, when my dad retired, I was living out-of-state. Besides, us Boomers march to our own drummer, don't we? So, to me, reinventing myself appealed to me. I wanted a new, worthwhile focus. I enrolled in a coaching program as a natural progression of my career, actually. I loved empowering people and helping them grow. In the process and building on that 'influence' in my profile, I created some podcasts for Boomers to expand their concept of what's possible. Doing more empowering, still!

In the process, I became impressed with a *Bigger* need—a need for a culture change around retirement—globally. With people turning 100 daily now, I sense a need to motivate and engage this resource for the good of our world.

Dr. Ken Dychtwald says over the next twenty years there will be about 3.9 trillion hours of time affluence for those 65 and over across the world. This is a new frontier that's begging for a solution. Like volunteering for the Peace Corps again!?

Now, I've created this resource and my signature system, The Effortless Vitality Plan, is to guide others in self-discovery, deeper wisdom, and to create their Essence statement. You've started the process by doing the suggested Action items here. Are you ready to step into understanding the inner DNA wisdom of you? When you feel your life flowing effortlessly from your heart, through your purpose, it feels like you are in love with life. It will make your heart sing!

Now, another retirement matter that needs to change is tackling the emotional side of retirement. The transition of leaving a long career, a competitive industry, or highly demanding overtime hours, can be hazardous to your health and no one talks about it!

All of the relationships with customers, teammates and colleagues are *gone*. You are no longer responsible for anything! You don't have any challenges to solve or fix. Nothing to achieve or accomplish. We don't realize how much *more* we get from our jobs than a paycheck. What will make you feel alive, focused and zoned in? Curious and excited?

The Effortless Vitality Plan addresses both this internal, deep self-discovery, and the external adjustments, so you have a healthy social, emotional, mental and spiritual plan. This vacuum and time freedom are confronted. You are supported and held accountable to make new decisions—new plans—since you are in charge. Without it, the isolation can too easily morph into depression, alcoholism and suicide. Maybe it starts with feeling sad or helpless. Aimlessness or a vague emptiness. Wasted time was *my* concern.

Courageously reach for the best in you. Fully honor your values. Fully expressing the essence of who you are will have a major impact on you and those around you. Don't you want that too? When you feel your life flowing effortlessly from your heart, through your purpose, it feels like you are in love with life. Fulfilled. Maybe even spiritual. Something our world is hungry for, I think. Thirsty.

You *can* do this 'cause you rock! You are worth it. When you get to be the boss of you, it's entirely your choice! I want you to feel complete, whole, satisfied, contented, happy and touching the rainbow with meaning and purpose. In love with LIFE. Wholehearted living.

Fulfillment was the topic of my interview with my colleague and friend DuAnne Redus in another podcast. She hosts her own radio show "On River Time" on KWVH. Our conversation had a river-time quality to it, in fact. When I asked how she defined fulfillment, she said "when I'm fulfilled, I'm calm inside my being. It's like I can just lie down inside my soul. Just let go deep inside and just be. Sometimes I lie on the floor and I just drop my arms and just breathe. So that gives me a physical sense. Another way I think about it is if we've seen hurricanes and tornadoes, but there's always that center *still* place. It's like being there for me. I can just let everything around me spin and I can just be in the center.

"Sometimes, when I think about being fulfilled, I'm also energized to co-create within my community. That fulfills me when I can connect with helping our community be stronger. Focusing on where the art lies, what feeds me spiritually; living close to nature does that for me. I need my dose of daily nature. I need my still-point, and I need something that motivates and energizes me to connect with them.

"If someone is different from me, like engineers and scientists' being very focused on detail, numbers or formulas, for them to be fulfilled might be different. They may need to feel safe and secure and knowledgeable about their field. It may look different. And that's what I think is curious, because fulfillment isn't the same to everyone.

"Someone who is very relational may feel unfulfilled right now (during the pandemic) because they can't meet their social needs. Then different music and Zoom help in connective ways. It's so individual and so subjective, what it means to truly be fulfilled."

When I asked DuAnne, What are some signals that one is either empty or full?, this was her response.

"When I'm full, I have a sense of humor. I can laugh at myself. I can look at a situation and kind of see something different about it. When I'm empty, I struggle. I might be critical. I might be blaming, I might be stuck in some judgment about something that takes me off track, but not when I relish or I'm in deep satisfaction.

"When I first retired and sold one of my businesses, I was amazed at how wonderful it was to sit in my chair and look out the window. To watch and listen to the birds. I had been so busy creating this business and jobs for people and taking care of employees, I didn't have enough time. That began to be a signal.

"Then I began to get more signals to slow down. My body was changing. Needed to honor and give it what it needs. Sometimes people are in slow-motion and actually need to energize themselves after sitting in a chair, on their computer, or watching TV.

"I always say, watch what gives you joy. How can you contribute to something that gives you joy? Because it's not all about me. It's about, *we*. What fills you up and we together can co-create something much bigger and more beautiful than we can even imagine yet."

So then I asked, What does it mean when people are out of balance?

"We can talk about balance in many ways. I can talk about just being able to align my posture because we work so much on media and computers. The heaviest part of our body is our head. And our whole physical structure becomes out of balance. What's basically out of balance is noticing emotionally: Is my mood good? Am I depressed? Am I sad? Noticing that emotional part of me.

"What do I need to pep myself up? Do I need to call somebody that can give me a mood lift? Maybe I need to learn something new, read a new book, have a different conversation. Join a book club. So, then I'm stimulated intellectually, mentally. Of course, spiritually is so different for everyone. I'll always do a little spiritual check. How am I, what's my spirit doing, what is my spirit saying to me? Do I need to do more meditation? Is my prayer time deep enough? What am I even praying about or meditating about? So, I see balance in this big spectrum of many dimensions of being physical, emotional, mental, and spiritual. And those are just little checks that we can have with ourselves. "

You might wonder, if people were more fulfilled, what would it look like?

Says DuAnne: "We can redefine what joy looks like in the future. I have a sense it's going to be focused more back to local communities and we have an aging population. As you and I know, these Baby Boomers are hitting 70 in large numbers. How do we take care of our elders? How do we honor our elders and ask them for their stories? How do we look back on our ancestry and bring that wisdom forward? Maybe it has been forgotten.

"I actually made a casserole this morning from somebody I knew was in my church during my youth. Her daughter put a recipe on Facebook last week in her mom's handwriting. And this morning, it kinda was like the history was there."

On our podcast, DuAnne told of a past event where she was at high-risk, and what her thought process was.

"Yes, huge risk. What I discovered was I did not trust myself. Wow! That's huge. It was. It set my life on a different course. I had trusted everybody around me and I had not trusted myself at the deepest level, but something needed to move me to a new place. I didn't know. So, everything I do now is if I hear a little voice that says, 'Don't do that, you might not, blah, blah, blah. Somebody might not like it,' I can go back to my gut, my heart and say, yes, I trust myself. I have the strength and the power to trust myself. I'm making good decisions for myself. Yes. There might be a tinge of risk and it's okay. I think a certain amount of that is also faith in yourself.

"Trust and faith. I'm not going to do something like jump off of that pole without a bollard and rope on. I'm not going to put myself in a situation I knowingly know is unsafe.

"Now, sometimes you may be in a circumstance that you didn't have control over. So sometimes it's like the pandemic and, I want more. I want to still be on my radio show. I still want it. So, what am I going to do? I'm going to create a way to be on the radio show. So, we found a way to prerecord it for a few weeks until it's safe to be back in the live studio. There's always the circumstance. And then what is my response to it?

"What is alive in you is supporting and encouraging you."

ACTIONS TO TAKE

- What whispers are you not listening to?

- What one thing can you do this week that's risky, vulnerable and puts a smile on your face?

- What have you let go of to get you to this place?

- What is your desire and the payoff, once you have it?

- Using an element of nature that captures your attention, imagine being IT! Describe yourself as being this object of nature, being as specific as possible, telling a story in the first person "I" voice.

- Journal how the richness of your soul is flowing through you.

- Where will you be in three years, if you don't start on a new journey now?

I'll know the next step,

once I take the first step.

EPILOGUE

In Chapter One, I shared my Essence statement. But what led up to it is a powerful story that helps flesh out this process more.

The first part happened when I lived in Irving, Texas. They hold a Mayfest the first weekend of May, and the year I went it was held outside around the football stadium in Irving. It was a three-day event, but I didn't go until Sunday afternoon. Little did I realize that vendors had already started packing up around three o'clock so I missed taking in the "whole" event. But back in the furthest corner was a booth I almost passed up. I *LOVE* unique stuff (and people) and it turns out this booth was showcasing the creative art of a geometry-teacher-turned-jeweler.

WHOA! Such an innovatively different design. He calls them sculptures and stackables. Ultimately unique. When the host suggested I try on one, I dared to say yes. When I did, something in my gut "moved!" I was shocked. Stunned. What's going on? I took them off and slipped them back on again. Same thing! It was a profound experience. I left knowing I absolutely needed to add them to my future and my dream board.

The second part goes back to when I was working in Everett, Washington. I've been a fan of self-help books over the years and one recommended that we write a descriptive statement about our contribution to our work team—as being something in nature. I still have it:

I am a rare jewel—a unique mosaic of precious and refined beauty. My talents and giftings are of the highest quality—being a strong, durable and superb contributor. Love sparkles through my eyes and countenance—I am a model of grace, beauty and love. I enhance any team or project. I add intensity, color and brilliance through excellence of execution, keen responsiveness, and delicate sensitivity. My leadership is captivating and carefully sought out. I am of rare value—creative, inspiring, distinctive and pleasingly superior. I am valuable, distinctive and very fine.

Then, the third part of this story is where I used this same descriptive paragraph as being the sculpture rings in nature and using its voice. (It has a distinct way of showing our heart!) In my coaching class, we added our favorite word(s): mine were synergy, color, collaboration, pure. After reading our paragraph to others to contribute additional objective suggestions, we selected our favorites and used them to form our statement. When we stood in front of our classmates, declaring our inner, true selves for the first time, it almost felt like a very sacred moment! Hushed and amazing. Often moving classmates and myself to tears.

Isn't this a perfect example of the mystery of life? I do expect to wear a stackable ring set when I am speaking someday, too!

Now, like I've said, I'm the perfect person to encourage and inspire *all* Boomers to an aspirational quest. There's gold in them Boomers, I declare! They've got a slew of time and it's about time for social profit or benefitting public organizations and foundations. There's room enough for everyone to create Good!

Let's find a team where we can pull in the same direction that really excites us. Leaving a legacy for the next generation is worthy of your focus now. Incorporate your desires for travel, purpose and new experiences together in this transformative growth season now.

I created an interactive video for you to begin your self-discovery using handouts that can be completed in a couple of hours or a couple of weeks.

Your next step is one-on-one coaching or joining a small group to engage in discussions and stand in your sacred moment.

Then, continuing with this group over six weeks, or working through another video alone, to address the remainder of your holistic retirement planning: social, emotional, mental, and a supportive foundation.

Check these out at EffortlessVitality.org and catch me on Facebook at Effortless Vitality and join my Retirement Well-Being group.

To schedule a free Virtual Coffee, here's my calendar link: http://bit.ly/EFVCoffeeChat

GOING DEEPER

CHAPTER ONE

Now, Discover Your Strengths by Marcus Buckingham & Donald O. Clifton, Ph.D.

What Color Is Your Parachute? by Richard N. Bolles

One Day University https://www.onedayu.com/aarp/

Life Reimagined https://www.aarp.org/about-aarp/life-reimagined/

Anne Frank quotes: "Whoever is happy will make others happy too. No one has ever become poor by giving. How wonderful it is that nobody need wait a single moment before starting to improve the world."

Elisa Hawkinson, author of *Calming your Chaos* and podcast guest. Organizing skills for life's road trip https://youtu.be/ppstPSE4O7<u>8</u>

Courage with Rev. Dr Robert "Bob" Nicholson podcast guest at https://www.spreaker.com/user/bbm_global_network/maximize-retirement-show-15

CHAPTER TWO

I've told many people how impressed I am by a lesson I learned from my sister, who knows what makes her happy! She lives in a farming community where it is pretty flat, windy and often dusty. When they started having a little discretionary time and money, she started looking around for something that would keep her husband busy. Over the years, she'd been collecting amazing photos of Mt Rainier which, on a clear day, they can see from her kitchen window. Ahh!

So, her search involved land for sale around Mt Rainier where it has lots of green; evergreen trees! Now, every three-day weekend they enjoy a respite in this evergreen haven in their 5th wheel with three slide-outs and the lovely firepit they made. That's where she is contented!

Why this impressed me so was how F-E-W people know what makes them happy! I can't say I really knew before my sister's example.

Just last week I heard a few people in Third World countries feel sorry for Americans, because they think they need so many things. For happiness? For temporary pleasure or immediate gratification?

I'm including some examples I think you will find helpful:

The JOY Diet – 10 Steps to a Happier Life by Martha Beck

Happy for No Reason: 7 Steps to Being Happy from the Inside Out, by Marci Shimoff

Tutoring is a Big Deal: investing in the success of future generations – Woody Clinard, podcast guest https://www.spreaker.com/user/bbm_global_network/maximize-retirement-show-20

Bonus Time – Alec Hill, podcast guest - https://youtu.be/sUyRfRTnusQ or his book *Living in Bonus Time – Surviving Cancer, Finding New Purpose*

9 Important Tips on Volunteering – John Barnett, podcast guest https://www.spreaker.com/user/bbm_global_network/maximize-retirement-show-9

CHAPTER THREE

"Overcoming Obstacles" with Carol Penney, podcast guest, talking about caregiving for her husband presented *an interesting new opportunity* when babysitting her grandson https://www.spreaker.com/user/bbm_global_network/maximize-retirement-show-19 Carol obstacles

"Better Angels" – provide thoughtful discussions among people of every political persuasion

Have a hobby that teaches your art or skill to intergenerational classes

thefriendshipforce.org – Take educational trips where you make friends around the world

SISTERS ON THE FLY camping https://www.youtube.com/watch?v
=UmiiXymWahU&feature=youtu.be&fbclid=IwAR21ACfJEO6fJRIv
KuA4oR07IqAcwpUeuUJ0CzeQ-OXS2_HfbMlgjZ8oF9g

"Playing for Change" – Stephanie Arroyo, podcast guest, who uses
soccer to help teach English, teamwork, exercise and health to people
of all ages: https://youtu.be/TZjbf5Z0jhs

Imagine speaking on behalf of homeless kids to learn team sports—
and head for college.

"Beating off Isolation" – Shelly Parks, podcast guest, with a career in
retirement living management, asked herself, 'How can we do this
better?' and now her goal is to ensure people have the opportunity
to live their best lives in community—through cohousing. Podcast:
https://youtu.be/kEd6Nt7BigQ

https://www.treehousefoundation.net/what-we-do/treehouse-
community/

https://www.wtvideo.com/video/21488/a-retirement-home-opens-
its-doors-to-children-from-an-orphanage-and-the-social-
experiment-is-an-undeniable-success

More resources:

https://www.psychologytoday.com/ca/blog/living-single/201610/
elder-orphans-real-problem-or-new-way-scare-singles

https://www.3rdactmagazine.com Aging with Confidence Magazine

Solo Traveler Groups &/or https://www.solo-travellers.com/

How to Live Forever – the enduring power of connecting the generations,
2018, by Marc Freedman

Keep On Keepin' On – A 2014 movie documenting the intergenerational
relationship between Clark Terry, a jazz legend, and Justin Kauflin, a
young blind piano jazz prodigy.

The Growing Season "Being fully present and focused" – Evan Briggs.
Director and podcast guest, documenting the intergenerational

Learning Center atProvidence Mount St. Vincent, a nursing home. https://youtu.be/6ivxIXQSRgc

Habitat Volunteering – John Budd, board president of Snohomish County (in Washington State) Habitat for Humanity, says there are thirty Global Village countries, and Care-A-Vanners in the US and Canada and women only projects. See www.habitat.org/rv

CHAPTER FOUR

Veteran/Military Aid with Michael Reagan, my podcast guest, is a great example of "Do what you did for charity." He is an artist who's created over ten thousand portraits of fallen veterans and first-responders. https://www.spreaker.com/user/bbm_global_network/maximize-retirement-show-11

Half-Time®: Moving from Success to Significance®, by Bob Buford

Confidence Lost/Confidence Found: How to Reclaim the Unstoppable You, by Kate McGuinness, formerly a high-flying LA lawyer, and my podcast guest, https://youtu.be/b729izYwubI

Happy & Rich? Podcast guest Eliyahu Jian, author of *The Laughing Billionaire: How to Become Rich & Happy* – https://youtu.be/WIMq0 SoVJOA

Leaving a nonfinancial legacy with podcast guest Robert Laura, a Michigan author, speaker, coach, and money manager. https://www.spreaker.com/user/bbm_global_network/maximize-retirement-show-5

Wisdom with podcast guest Jeff Rubin, author, speaker and positive aging advocate https://www.spreaker.com/user/bbm_global_network/maximize-retirement-show-10

Encore.org, founded by Marc Freedman, focuses on intergenerational solutions to pressing social problems from literacy to loneliness by bridging divides and collaborating across generations to create a better future together.

America's Future Corps – the new Peace Corps article from Lustre https://www.lustre.net/home/2016/5/13/americas-future-corps-an-idea?rq=america%27s%20future%20corps

Age-Friendly Cities – Dr. Frank Caro, podcast guest https://www.spreaker.com/user/bbm_global_network/maximize-retirement-show-18_

CHAPTER FIVE

Letting loose of constricting things with Stacey Tompkins, podcast guest talking about her El Camino journey: https://youtu.be/XPx2Snu5QoI

Serving our Communities with Dave Teitzel, podcast guest https://www.spreaker.com/user/bbm_global_network/maximize-retirement-show-21 Dave T

The Soul of Money – Transforming Your Relationship with Money and Life, by Lynne Twist

Disrupt You! Master Personal Transformation, Seize Opportunity, and Thrive in the Era of Endless Innovation, by Jay Samit

CHAPTER SIX

Music is Medicine for the body – Gary Malkin, composer of Graceful Passages - https://youtu.be/MV-G-mFVOXw

Where's the original? – Bruce Cryer, author of *From Chaos to Coherence – The Power to Change Performance* and Renaissance Human Newsletter- https://youtu.be/E-zVz3lfFXQ

Stretching the limits of who we are - Dori Mintzer podcast guest & author - https://youtu.be/DKC1nyTj5k0

Follow your passion: Gregg Levoy, author of *Callings – Finding and Following An Authentic Life* and *Vital Signs – Discovering and Sustaining Your Passion for Life*, podcast guest https://youtu.be/c_wtYVAtnIg

Liberating Greatness: the Whole Brain Guide to Living an Extraordinary Life, by Hal Williamson with Sharon Eakes. An amazing autobiography – from being slow in school, through alcoholism, becoming a patent attorney, and creating the Pathways to Greatness seminar series.

Building strong communities through sports – Corky Frady, founder of Let's Sack Cancer Foundation, podcast guest - https://youtu.be/e-pDfbD5Hqc

We are changing communities around the world with education https://unstoppablefoundation.org/ *Unstoppable Women*, by Cynthia Kersey.

The Soul of Money, by Lynne Twist + free offer "7 Steps to Free Yourself from Money Stress"

Money talks. Are you listening?

Love Money. Money Loves You, by Sarah McCrum.

 Rich or Wealth Strategy?

The Rich Life: Ten Investments for True Wealth, by Beau Henderson, podcast guest: https://youtu.be/lP341Q_S57E

The Laughing Billionaire: How to Become Rich and Happy, by Eliyahu Jian, podcast guest: https://youtu.be/WIMq0SoVJOA

WOMEN GIVING:

Colleen S. Willoughby is an American philanthropist who is credited with creating the model of collective giving grantmaking, which is commonly referred to as *giving circles.* She is the founder and former president of the Washington Women's Foundation and current director of Global Women Partners in Philanthropy.

A **giving circle** is a form of participatory philanthropy where groups of individuals donate their own money or time to a pooled fund, decide together where to give these away to charity or community projects and, in doing so, seek to increase their awareness of and engagement in the issues covered by the charity or community project.

Many circles, in addition to donating their money, also contribute their time and skills to support local causes.

This inspired a group of New York City ladies to start their own: https://wellmetgroup.org/

CHAPTER SEVEN

Foundations and Compassion – Blaine Bartlett, author of *Compassionate Capitalism: Journey to the Soul of Business*, podcast guest along with his wife, Cynthia Kersey, author of *Unstoppable* and *Unstoppable Women* – https://www.spreaker.com/user/bbm_global_network/maximize-retirement-show-24

Fulfillment vs Out-of-Balance – DuAnne Redus, podcast guest, author and creator of EASE Alignment Process – https://youtu.be/jjB5ry0y1s8

Heaven on Earth? –guest Martin Rutte, author of *Project Heaven on Earth – The 3 simple questions that will help you change the world … easily* – https://youtu.be/Z3zwWLbogPs

Your Holiness: Discover the Light Within, by Debbie Ford.

AARP purpose prize – https://www.aarp.org/about-aarp/purpose-prize/ You live. You learn. You give back. No one knows this better than people ages 50 and older, who have spent decades accumulating a wealth of knowledge that only life experience can bring. Armed with this wisdom, they are a powerhouse of innovation tackling some of the greatest societal challenges of our time and inspiring others to do the same.

The AARP® Purpose Prize® award supports AARP's mission by honoring extraordinary people ages 50 and older who tap into the power of life experience to build a better future for us all.

"The AARP Purpose Prize is all about a new story of aging—focusing on experience and innovation and the idea that our aging population is an untapped resource full of possibilities," said AARP CEO Jo Ann

Jenkins. "AARP Purpose Prize winners and nominees are role models. They are makers and doers who are out there creating new solutions that make the world a better place for people of all ages." https://www. aarp.org/about-aarp/purpose-prize/previous-honorees/

Remembering Wellness, Purpose, Abundance – Dr Sharnael Wolverton Sehon ND - https://swiftfire.org/

Gary Burnison, CEO of Korn Ferry, says, "Our firm's research shows that purposes and values that benefit others are more meaningful than those that focus only on one's self and one's own pleasure, profit, or advancement. We must first look within: here we *find our gifts*. (Then) We must *give our gifts*. https://www.kornferry.com/insights/articles/ the-courage-to-find-meaning

EPILOGUE

Positive Intelligence – Why Only 20% of Teams and Individuals Achieve Their True Potential and How You Can Achieve Yours, by Shirzad Chamine. 2012. Covers the topic of Mental Fitness.

FRESH COURAGE

Passion has the
ability to light
a spark in
all of us.

ACKNOWLEDGMENTS

The Spark inside each one of us; the convergence zone of God, my talent and my passion.

Dr. Ken Dychtwald and Robert Morison, authors of *What Retirees Want: A Holistic View of Life's Third Age*. Their work gives backbone to much of my work; the fuel for the task that needs to be done in helping Boomers find their purpose.

Of course, there are many hands that touch and improve, talented ones that add shine and sparkle to the end product. And, friends who have lent support along the way. Rosemary Macauley is such a dynamite friend along my growth journey. Then there are the leaders, pastors and friends who help us grow and learn. Many of these were part of Fellowship of Christian Adult Singles (FOCAS) and the conferences we hosted in the mid-'80s in Seattle.

The colleagues who were in the learning process with me: Lynn Scarborough, Diana Needham, Juliana Van Buskirk. Plus, all the authors I've learned from. Thank you. My podcast guests for contributing their wisdom, knowledge and experiences.

I am so inspired by Martha Beck, Rosamund Zander, and Cynthia Kersey.

My Boomer MeetUp group who gave me the practice, support and confidence that I might be onto something here.

Serenade KING FM 91.8 Ultimate Classics #4\Serenade.wma

Josh Groban and his recording of "You Raise Me Up."

My launch team: Martin Rutte, DuAnne Redus, Fran Fisher, Pete Finlon, Melissa Ternes, Cris Cathey and Michelle Seifert.

Do more of
what brings
you joy.

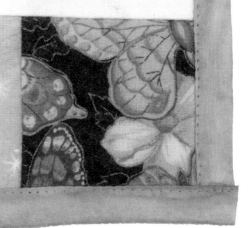

ABOUT THE AUTHOR

Sharon Rolph inspires, collaborates and motivates others with ideas, possibilities and potential. If you can dream it, it is possible. People were introduced to her work through her *What Do I Want to Do in Retirement* workshops. Then she transitioned into podcasting: Maximize Retirement (audio only) and FRESH COURAGE (both audio and video), which are available on her business website EffortlessVitality.org. She is an analyst, communicator and listener; a systems thinker, maximizer and optimist who *loves* creating synergy.

Sharon expresses her creative side through patchwork quilting. Her love of sewing and love of color is showcased in her quilts and postcard-size wall hangings. The fabric art is created in the Seattle area where she strives for a WOW factor with color, a little shine or inspirational wisdom. She likes to use something that might catch the sun and sparkle for a moment. Each item is as unique as Sharon is and some can be found at ETSY in the QuiltedPetunia store. (ETSY store: QuiltedPetunia)

Sharon grew up in the Puget Sound and Eastern Washington, where she pursued education in Behavioral Science, Administration and Technical Arts. She worked for Boeing in Tukwila as a Business Process Analyst, for nineteen years for GTE in Everett and Tampa, and three years in Dallas, Texas, for USPS and IBM.

Her travels have taken her to Alaska, Nashville, Switzerland, Italy and Australia. Now, Holland, New Zealand and Costa Rica are on her bucket list.

Sharon has two sisters, thirteen nieces and nephews, and challenges herself each year to make their Christmas gifts. A unique legacy, of sorts.

Fresh Courage
IN RETIREMENT

WHAT IF YOU COULD IMAGINE...

- Bringing Long-Dormant Dreams to Reality
- Saying Goodbye to Stress, Haste and Waste
- Discovering the Difference You Could Make in Someone Else's Life
- Traveling to New Places, New Cultures
- Making Friends around the Globe
- Finding Unique Ways to Share Your Whims and Wisdom
- Sharing and Trading Stories with New Pals
- Smiling and Laughing as a Daily Routine and, finally...
- <u>Loving Every Minute of a Wholehearted New Chapter in Life</u>

Behavioral scientist and life coach Sharon Rolph uncovers these and other joyful benefits for Baby Boomers reaching an age where their ancestors may have settled into lethargy and boredom.

As Rolph points out, there are so many ways to transform your life with novel undertakings that will expand your mind – and your heart. Many retirees want to stay useful and relevant but don't know how.

Says Rolph: "Without a boss, there is a new lease on life; nobody is holding us back. What's possible, now? Start exploring options that energize you with my suggested Actions to Take. Retirees want fun, stimulating, nourishing, purposeful and transformative things to do. Be curious about what that is for you."

• • • • • • • • • • • • • • • •

"...a conversational dialog of compelling and refreshing insight into the dynamics of a sometimes tasking and stressful professional life."

Mark Reynolds
International Business Strategist

"If you're a retiree or soon to become one, imagine having your own unique, creative, inspiring, legacy-leaving project that directly impacts people, planet and Life itself. With this book you no longer have to imagine...you can make it real."

Martin Rutte
Founder
www.ProjectHeavenOnEarth.com

SELF-HELP/RETIREMENT

$15.95
ISBN 978-1-7339618-9-9
51595>
9 781733 961899

Published by
EDK Books

Distributed by
EDK Distribution, LLC